Among the Angels of Memory

Entre los ángeles de la memoria

"The Angel of Memory" by Natalia Nakazawa

Among the Angels
Entre los ángeles
of Memory
de la memoria

MARJORIE AGOSÍN

English Translation
by Laura Rocha Nakazawa

Introduction by Robert Bonazzi

San Antonio, Texas
2006

Among the Angels of Memory / Entre los ángeles de la memoria
© 2006 by Marjorie Agosín

Introduction © 2006 by Robert Bonazzi

Cover painting, "Tricorn," by Yevgenia Nayberg. Used by permission.
Frontis illustration, "The Angel of Memory," © 2005 by
Natalia Nakazawa. Used by permission.

The translation of *Entre los ángeles de la memoria* into English was
made possible in part by a generous grant from Wellesley College.

First Wings Press Edition

ISBN-10: 0-916727-13-0
ISBN-13: 978-0-916727-13-0

Wings Press
627 E. Guenther
San Antonio, Texas 78210
Phone/fax: (210) 271-7805
On-line catalogue and ordering:
www.wingspress.com

Library of Congress Cataloging-in-Publication Data

Agosín, Marjorie.
  Among the angels of memory = Entre los ángeles de la memoria /
written by Marjorie Agosín ; translated from the Spanish by Laura
Rocha Nakazawa.-- 1st Wings Press ed.
       p. cm.
  ISBN 0-916727-13-0 / 978-0-916727-13-0
  I. Title: Entre los ángeles de la memoria. II. Nakazawa, Laura
Rocha. III. Title.
  PQ8098.1.G6A76 2006
  861'.64--dc22
                                                  2005034339

*Except for fair use in reviews and/or scholarly
considerations, no portion of this book may be
reproduced without the permission of the*

Contents

Author's Preface	*vii*
Translator's Note	*x*
The Exiled Angels of Memory: An Introduction by Robert Bonazzi	*xi*

The Old World • El Viejo Mundo

Helena Broder: Angel of Memory	*3*
Helena Broder, Vienna, 1939	*4*
Helena Broder	*10*
Helena Broder	*11*
Noche de Viena	*12*
Viennese Night	*13*
Maletín de viaje	*14*
Traveling Bag	*15*
El impredecible tren del norte	*18*
Unpredictable Northern Train	*19*
Como el color de la niebla	*24*
Like the Color of Fog	*25*
Confesión de los austriacos	*26*
Austrian Confession	*27*
Girasol herido	*28*
Wounded Sunflower	*29*
Sobre Terezin, Helena Broder solloza	*34*
Helena Broder Sobs over Terezin	*35*
Primas	*38*
Cousins	*39*
Los ángeles inclinados de Helena Broder	*48*
The Leaning Angels of Helena Broder	*49*
Llegas a Praga	*50*
Arrival in Prague	*51*
Tus pasos sobre la nieve de Praga	*54*
Your Footsteps in the Snow of Prague	*55*
El gólem de Praga	*56*
The Golem of Prague	*57*
Rue de Rosier	*60*
Rue de Rosier	*61*
Huellas	*64*
Traces	*65*

The New World • El Nuevo Mundo

1939	72
1939	73
Chile, 1939	74
Chile, 1939	75
Creí que eras un ángel, Helena	78
I Thought you Were an Angel, Helena	79
Helena sueña con el viento	80
Helena Dreams of the Wind`	81
El cuaderno de direcciones de Helena	82
Helena's Address Book	83
Los sueños de Helena Broder	84
The Dreams of Helena Broder	85
Helena Broder contempla el cielo	86
Helena Broder Contemplates the Sky	87
Diminutos son tus pies, Helena	90
Your Feet Are Tiny, Helena	91
Helena Broder conmemora el blanco y negro	92
Helena Broder Commemorates the Black-and-White	93
Las Odiseas de Helena	94
Helena's Odysseys	95
Los mapas de Helena	98
Helena's Maps	99
La carta de Helena Broder	102
Helena Broder's Letter	103
Conversaciones con Dios y Helena Broder	108
Conversations with God and Helena Broder	109
La ceremonia del adiós	112
The Ritual of Goodbye	113
Ella	116
She	117
Tu rostro	120
Your Face	121
Tus manos	126
Your Hands	127
La casa de la memoria	128
The House of Memory	129
Les Milles	134
Les Milles	135
Pesaj en Chile	138
Passover in Chile	139
Torah	144

Torah	*145*
Sukkot	*146*
Sukkot	*147*
La noche de Auschwitz	*150*
Night at Auschwitz	*151*
Imaginar un navío	*154*
Imagine a Ship	*155*
Traducir es otra forma de amar	*160*
Translating Is Another Way of Loving	*161*
El árbol de la memoria	*166*
The Tree of Memory	*167*
Sebastopol	*172*
Sebastopol	*173*
Las cosas olvidadas	*176*
Forgotten Things	*177*
La tierra	*180*
The Earth	*181*
Paz	*184*
Peace	*185*
Jerusalén	*188*
Jerusalem	*189*
Biographical Notes	*198*

Author's Preface

I belong to a lineage of traveling women who were always ready to take flight, women with feet like wings. My great-grandmothers invariably had a suitcase under their beds where they kept their most precious objects: candles to illuminate the growing darkness, salt to accompany each meal, and sugar to sweeten sorrows. I grew up surrounded by these travelers, these astonishing and diaphanous creatures, always ready to go to the most remote corners of the Earth. I am an inheritor of these travelers who, at the turn of the century, crossed over rivers and oceans from Odessa, to Turkey, to Marseilles, to finally arrive at their ultimate destination, the port of Valparaíso, with its generous harbor, resembling the smiling face of my wandering ancestors. I am also an inheritor of other travelers who passed through the cities of Vienna, Prague and Hamburg while Europe was burning. They also arrived at the port of Valparaíso in the middle of a flowering spring to find happiness at the end of the world.

For these travelers, Chile was the site of permanence and the landscape of refuge. They all remained the rest of their lives in this luminous country. Growing up surrounded by the fables and myths of those journeys, I understood that language was my house of memory. The Spanish language has always been with me throughout my many diasporas. The alphabet was my home; with it I made necklaces, constructed histories, talked about many things.

Through my writings, that I call maps of memory, I have recreated the history of my mother in a memoir titled *A Cross and a Star*, and later I recreated my father's memory in *Always from Somewhere Else*. I also went back, even further, to evoke my great-grandmother Helena Broder's journey starting one night in Vienna until the night in which she left for Hamburg to find her final destination in the port of Valparaíso. These poems, gathered in a collection called *The Angel of Memory* (Wings Press, 2001), honor the daring travels of my great-grandmother, her tenacity, audacity and vision, which allowed her to save her life in that terrible year of 1939 when Hitler annexed Austria, and Kristallnacht altered the rhythm of history.

    The Angel of Memory tells her story and mine, as well as that of the 20th century with its lessons of violence and evil. I felt compelled to return to the Vienna she left sixty years ago to find her; to smell her perfume among the old dresses of ancient ladies, or to imagine her buying flowers on Fridays. I found my great-grandmother in the memories that my mother and I together recreated and strung as if they were the most precious of necklaces. Memory has its own rhythm, a secret and intimate melody. It moves through the most isolated rooms, and then reappears, luminous and near, when we think to have lost it. Yet, it is the desire to bring it to life, to rescue it, that dominates my history and the poetry of these pages.

    The Angel of Memory inhabits the memories of Helena Broder, her morning walks, her rose garden, the arrival of Kristallnacht, the humiliations suffered from her neighbors, the arrival at the port of Valparaíso, and the impossibility of a return to a burning Europe.

    While writing this book of poems I realized that the sacred language of poetry could conquer death and oblivion; that the memory of Helena Broder belongs now to me and to everyone. As I had spoken through writing, she had returned to the house and had made her peace with history.

    This new collection, *Among the Angels of Memory,* is a more daring path to challenge oblivion, to suggest that it is always possible to return to beloved people and places. Here I recover many voices, the poet recreating her great-grandmother's steps, but also my own in the process of sensing the memories of others and participating in the post-memory of them. This also allows me to bring onto the stage my language, and the memories of my mother who told them to me and helped me evoke Helena Broder's history. Memory finds itself at the center of this coexistence with these texts.

The reader will understand that the branches of memory roam through the crevices of dreams. History and memory move through a lineal time, interposing themselves outside a clearly delineated chronology. They move through time, zigzagging the march of history. They return to the space of dreams, possibilities and ruins. They are poems and voices engaged in conversation, listening and caressing each other. Poetry exercises its hypnotic powers over them. The magic of intuition and enchantment surrounding them allows them to live inside and outside of History.

These poems should be read as a continuation of *The Angel of Memory* because in responding to that first angel, they have attempted to elucidate the possibilities of becoming voices speaking with each other. But above all, they exhort us not to remain indifferent to the call of history.

– Marjorie Agosín
Wellesley College

Translator's Note

Translation responds to the strict demands of the craft, yet also constitutes an authentic transformation. More than finding accurate equivalents from one language to another, a sensitive translation seeks to recreate in the target language the same emotions and associations enjoyed by readers in the original language. In translating Marjorie Agosín's beautifully evocative and richly visual poems, I have tried to enter into her world, like an explorer into a new landscape. Her eloquent words and images have illuminated my path and guided my steps. It is my hope that these translated versions of her poems can equally allow English language readers the same richness, measured rhythm, and love for life that she has expressed.

In this process I feel privileged to have had the wise, perceptive and careful reading of Jonathan Cohen, the noted translator of Latin American poetry, who patiently looked over the manuscript, making insightful comments and suggestions. His observations regarding some of the poems that dealt with specifically Jewish religious themes, such as Passover, Torah or Sukkot, showed me hidden meanings of the ritual that enhanced my understanding of the original poems. Thank you, Jonathan, for your support and kind guidance.

I would like to thank Marjorie Agosín for her trust, encouragement and deep friendship. Working on her poetry is always a journey into hope, empathy and a deep sense of humanity.

– Laura Rocha Nakazawa

The Exiled Angels of Memory
An Introduction

Robert Bonazzi

A*mong the Angels of Memory,* an expanded sequel to the Wings Press limited edition of *The Angel of Memory*, takes a different form and offers new poems through a fresh translation by Laura Rocha Nakazawa. Like the previous book, this one concerns the life of Helena Broder – Agosín's maternal great-grandmother and her "messenger angel" – who allows the poet "to answer questions about the dead and the living."

    This new portrait reveals an even richer Helena, beginning with the poet's prose poem in her great-grandmother's own voice, a transforming text that evokes Helena's thoughts on leaving the Old World "of horrific goose-steps" and crossing the Pacific to the port of Valparaíso, Chile – her entry into the New World, where "lights were like dancing fireflies and the savage flowers bent to welcome us into a twilight of unexplored dreams." At the end of this piece, Helena acknowledges Frida, Agosín's mother, as the one who "will remember with precision the date of your arrival in Chile, in 1939." Frida will also "recall the translucent tulle bonnet flowing in the wind, the delicate neckline that insinuated the softness of your neck, still fresh, your delicate breasts, your silver candelabra and the garnet bracelet that has inherited the fate of all our migrations, and now rests peacefully in the hands of your great-grand-daughter," the poet Marjorie Agosín, who continues to be the guardian of memory for her fascinating family of Jewish exiles.

    Earlier memoirs, which concern her mother (*A Cross and A Star*), her father (*Always From Somewhere Else*), and herself (*The Alphabet in My Hands*), were composed of impressionistic vignettes. These first three memoirs had as their central conflict the rise and ruthless rule of Pinochet's CIA-supported regime in Chile, when her family emigrated to the United States shortly before the political assassination of President Salvador Allende, a family friend. For her parents – double exiles from Europe and South America – life in the States has been difficult in the psychic sense. Like their daughter, they have not embraced American culture or the English language with the same passion that they became integrated into the Spanish idiom of Chilean culture, although they have endured virulent anti-Semitism everywhere.

Raised in Santiago, Agosín continues to remember and to write in Spanish, even though she speaks English, and has taught at Wellesley for nearly two decades. However, Agosín teaches what she lives – the literature and human rights struggle of Latin America – a cultural lineage of which her own work has become an organic part.

The lyric heir of Chilean Nobel laureates and poets of the people, Gabriela Mistral and Pablo Neruda, Agosín has been recognized by the United Nations and Jewish organizations for her human rights activism. She has written tirelessly about the victims of 20th century violence, always with emphasis on the lives of women and children; and she has edited significant anthologies of writing by women, including *Women, Gender and Human Rights*, *Uncertain Travelers* and *A Map of Hope*.

This new memoir, like *The Angel of Memory*, first returns to the European Holocaust of World War II, where many of Agosín's relatives died in concentration camps and from where the fortunate ones escaped to Chile. She writes again of Helena Broder as one who

>   knew how to give destiny the slip,
>   how to predict the right moment to fly
>   in 1939, dressed as if
>   for an evening party. . . .

In the Introduction to *The Angel of Memory*, she recalled her own childhood as "Eight years of being an inquisitive young girl, daring to penetrate the forbidden questions, or the body of blazing memory." This internal landscape of family intimacies and secrets, of brushing Helena's hair, of eyeing the quiet room where her great-grandmother lived in Chile resonates with the old world's past. "Your room was not like a Chilean's room, my mother used to say. The blankets, the water jars, the inkwell and the luminous candles were not from this America. You brought your Vienna and its lilacs with you. . . . Without a doubt, you were a queen among us, with your magician's gaze and your wise sayings."

The poems in *Among the Angels of Memory* are divided into two main sections – before and after Helena's passage to Chile – and navigate the memoir from various vantages. Those before departure ("The Old World") concern the human side of the Holocaust and include portraits of Nazi functionaries rather than descriptions of Hitler's war. The tone tends toward ironic understatement and carries a deep sense of grief.

The utter predictability of "Unpredictable Northern Train" echoes a clear example of her tone. The train conductor, who does his job, acts as a horrendous symbol of cold cruelty, rationalization and denial.

> Like a darkened traveler,
> the train conductor
> confident, precise,
> checks that all passengers,
> including the shorn women,
> those dressed like brides and death,
> and the gasping elders,
> board this train
> that will deliver them
> to the place from which
> there is no return,
> to the place of nameless horrors

> to the most inexplicable secret
> the secret we all know.
>
> The train conductor
> is well respected for his work,
> deserves a medal
> for his punctuality.
> He knows the fate of those trains:
> the stations of blue gas,
> the home of that fog,
> that silence beyond all silences,
> where bodies burn like dead flowers.

The conductor "considers himself noble in this obedience," because

> After all,
> it is only Jews who travel
> on these trains
> and it is his duty,
> his passionate vocation,
> to make the Jews disappear.

The reference to the Jews who disappeared on such trains reverberates in the poet's memory with "los desaparecidos" – those who disappeared from Pinochet's Chile, either tossed into unmarked graves or pushed from US helicopters into the Pacific Ocean.

Disappearance into non-identity seems to be the paranoid pattern of all dictatorships: If there are no victims, there is no enemy. In all the post-World War II slaughters, victims have not been imprinted with a number, or even counted at all, as in the denial of the US military as to the "collateral damage" otherwise known as civilians in Iraq.

Most of us do not have first-hand knowledge of unspeakable atrocities, but Agosín's family does – and she speaks about the unspeakable in one book after another. A powerful poem ("Cousins") concerns the aftermath of just such an event, about her first cousins who were gassed in Auschwitz.

> On holy days
> their seats were vacant
> and my father, with his sacred cup,
> invoked their names:
> Julia, Sonia, Silvia.

The cousins' names become a litany in a poem filled with scant remnants of their lives, which were lost in history – but not to memory.

> I too came to love them,
> was comforted to see
> their handwriting
> on frayed postcards
> from Vienna, then
> Prague, and later still
> the cities with austere names.

Those "cities with austere names" began with the dreaded Auschwitz,

> ... where there are no calendars,
> where there is no memory,
> where there is no voice,
> where women keep silent,
> are shorn.

The poet does not "know how to remember them" and feels that she does "not deserve life/without them." Halfway through this narrative poem, Agosín gives way to the anguish of direct statement and breaks the skin of the poem to confess that:

> Telling you this story
> distresses me,
> I can only say it in a poem
> as I am unable to tell it to anyone.
> I don't want to hear things like:
> "Again, the Jews and their memories."
> "That happened years ago."
> "I don't know anything about that."
> That is how they talked when
> the neighbor, the grandfather,
> and his small grandchildren were abducted.

Is anyone listening? Then why such callused remarks blaming the victims of prejudice? Because the patterns of prejudice are universal, and must be consciously overcome individually. We also hear from those who claim to be free of bigotry: "Here we go again," complains the dominant majority about minorities, "as if segregation or the holocaust were still going on. What are Blacks and Jews crying about anyway? It's the Muslims and Arabs who get the brunt of abuse these days."

In truth, every group has been victimized at some time in history and all nations have a history of blood on their hands. But that does not change Agosín's view of human rights. "One is born with human rights," she writes in *An Absence of Shadows*, thus one is sacredly connected to all living things." For example, she never rationalizes the Israeli or US occupations; rather she stands in solidarity with Palestinian and Iraqi civilians, as well as with all victims of war and prejudice, because "when human rights are violated, so is the sacredness of the world."

No matter the locale or time-frame of these violations – from her book of poems, *Dear Anne Frank*, to those about Latin American atrocities in *An Absence of Shadows* – Agosín remembers and writes. In the first part of *Among the Angels of Memory*, she declares in "The Golem of Prague":

> I know that we live in memory,
> or in the metaphor of memory,
> or in a memory that allows neither oblivion
> nor promises,
> or in the imagination of a memory
> that plays with distance,
> a small somber bell sounding
> upon the kingdom of the dead.

Among exiled family members, memory evolved through living stories. In "Memory and Exile" she writes: "The exile of our ancestors managed to stir my imagination to the rhythms of solitude and it was possible for me to build lives, alternating melodies and words. Exile became fundamental to a form of writing that had begun in a closely guarded fashion but which was filled with a powerful desire to create life."

Her own exile from Chile as a teenager became inhabited by memory and expressed through the medium of her Spanish language. "Exile from a world to which I never had access became the essence of my writing," she points out. "That is to say, it facilitated the possibility of invention, of doubt, of daydreaming.... Literature and its aesthetic expression of language were the most powerful ways to recover what had been lost." She means a dynamic, evolving memory, not merely a static recounting of facts. "I invented the family I never had and those whose lives I assumed had ended in a forest of barbed wires, dead or feigning death. I made them come to life, gave them hair and voices."

"Traces" – the final poem from "The Old World" section of *Among the Angels of Memory* – begins:

> More than a memory,
> or the place where memory lives,
> like a texture,
> more than a presence,

> among the phantoms and flickering spirits,
> in the wandering heart of night,
> among the flames
> in that unsettled place,
> I found traces,
> only traces,
> cast-off, shipwrecked syllables,
> shattered alphabets.

From these traces, left by those who lit a flame or picked a flower, she creates in poetry her "lucid testaments of history," remaining one who "walks among the rubble/and listens to a lament,/a cadence,/traces,/a name,/a people who cry out,/a people who pray /and are resplendant."

"The New World" contains intimate texts about Helena, including personae poems in Helena's "voice" and poems from the poet's double viewpoints – some based on childlike experiences with Helena, others being mature reflections derived from Frida Agosín's family stories.

The opening transitional texts are the brief "1939" (quoted earlier) and "Chile, 1939," which closes on "the angels of memory/arrive at your feet." Then follows a suite of unfolding variations on the émigré's life in Chile, evoking Helena's thoughts and dreams, focusing on tangible symbols – photographs, maps and an address book.

"I Thought You Were an Angel, Helena" observes "a stranger among your own / belongings," and leads to a child's ghostly question and tender response.

> Who were you looking for, so light and small,
> in your white nightgown,
> with your tiny lantern?
>
> I thought you were an angel
> and I played at discovering
> each one of your messages,

> messenger of intense life,
> of the frail memory,
> a gardener of nocturnal flowers.

Most of these poems question the unknown and some – like "Helena Broder Contemplates the Sky" – venture an answer in Helena's voice:

> It was an imaginary city,
> the sky,
> where nested the names
> of the dead and the living.

"Helena's Maps" creates a startling reversal – identifying entirely with Helena's dislocation but actually speaking of the poet's lost Chile:

> Stunned, tied to the amazing
> circling of my hand,
> I look for my country.
> The map lies
> on a decrepit, distant table
> in the lost dominions of exile.
>
> I search for my rivers
> disfigured and yellow
> in this fragile geography of exile.
> I cannot find my beloved Andes,
> scattered and blue.

Several stanzas later her bewilderment returns, ending the poem with a symbol that identifies her as a school girl in Santiago.

> Stunned, I find myself
> in a borrowed, fugitive geography
> that does not belong to me.
> . . . .

> I am searching with maddened faith
> for what became of that house
> with doors full of happiness
> and I seek out my blue school uniform,
> dead on some flimsy chair.

The vocabulary of exile – its "lost dominions" and "borrowed, fragile geography" – are upheld by real but wounded objects: that map "on a decrepit, distant table," that school uniform on "some flimsy chair." Even as exile implies vulnerability and diminishment, living grief creates the persistence of memory and only forgetfulness signifies ultimate loss.

"Writing from exile must be a permanence, constantly articulating the present, the past, the memories and lack of memories" – Agosín clarifies in "Memory and Exile" – "as a way of being and living in a world where the possibility of remembering and being a witness is not outside of history but a part of history." The mantra of "Never Forget" still rings loud and clear, for without the memories of Holocaust witnesses that record of terror would have been less complete. We can also hear versions of that mantra from the Palestinian and Iraqi communities today; and there should be no doubt that the Israeli and US occupations will not be soon forgotten, no matter what long-range outcome prevails on paper.

"Conversations with God and Helena Broder" looks at such madness:

> I am a Jew
> wrestling with you
> a Jew
> who does not understand
> why in my eyes burn
> the villages of Lithuania,
> the cells of Terezin,
> the piled up bodies
> of Rwanda.

Since Helena Broder did not live to hear of Rwanda, we know that the poet has taken on her voice. But God is silent, and "His presence/had no answers,/but questions." Still she believes in "the strongest proof/of survival,/the miracle of being..." Helena survived eight years in Chile, and in "The Ritual of Goodbye" the young Agosín cannot attend the funeral. "You are going, Helena Broder," she writes, "and the doves will not return to the balcony,/only the absence of your steps,/shall invoke your presence." Yet in the "absence" a "presence" in memory remains. But that "presence" becomes transcribed in "The House of Memory":

> At dawn,
> the space of poetry comes
> in the clear hours.
> My hand feels this divine
> presence,
> humble, fertile glory.
> My fingers glide over the words,
> as if each one of them
> were a love story,
> a fragrance among syllables.
> I knit words,
> luminous waves over the page,
> calmly, I take dictation.
> And you, on the other side of the words,
> in the resonant clarity of light,
> smile.
>
> Poetry is the story of love,
> eternal flame
> to mitigate the solitude of those who love
> each other in the dark.

A companion lyric that counters silence, loneliness and darkness – "Translating Is Another Way of Loving" – appears later. From memory to poetry to translation: All bridges for love but never hatred, crossing the divides of time, place, language. Agosín "translates" Helena's Viennese spirit-presence in Spanish: "I translate without oblivion,/only presences of one voice over another,/like a hand that resembles/a garden in shadows/reborn in a different light." The poem evokes love and living in every image – "in this cluster of human/ voices,/ constellations without borders." – and "From one hand in love with the quartz of letters,/the supportive republic of writing."

It would be impossible to discuss Agosín's work if one could not read Spanish, or if it had not been brought into English by many translators. In a *MultiCultural Review* interview, she spoke of a covenant with Spanish and with those who have translated her work into English.

> I felt that without language I had no voice; I had no identity; I was nothing. It took many years until I learned – I don't want to say mastered but was able to communicate in – the English language, and became a person in English. Then I acquired a sense of self in a new language. That to me was very important for without translations we are speechless. But what I also learned about translation was that even though I became someone once I learned English, I did not want to lose my Spanish self, which was really my Spanish language, because you are what you speak.

Later in the same interview she equated memory to a form of translation:

> But memory is also very complicated because it consists of what one chooses to remember. So perhaps a translator has to choose the right words, and that again makes translation an act of choices. [However] the translation of poetry is the translation of the spirit. So a translator does not simply translate; the translator also becomes that voice. To become someone else you

have to be in love with someone else. And in that sense I strongly believe that translations are acts of love. If it were not for that act of love of the translator, great literature would not exist in other languages. To write in Spanish is a gesture of survival, and because of translation my memory has now become a part of the memory of others.

As Agosín has stated clearly, the predominant sources of memory for this book were the stories her mother Frida told about Helena, as well as the poet's childhood reflections. Gathered together, such intimate sources provide textured remembrances over time via free associations, exquisite impressions and startling images. In *Among the Angels of Memory*, these deeply personal poems have taken on narrative forms in most cases, as Agosín remains a faithful story-teller, exploring every branch and leaf of her luminous family tree in memoirs, essays, short stories and poems. Yet the narrative texts of this new book are more concerned with "the story of love" than with family chronology, and imbued with a subtle sense of the "presence" of loved ones rather than cataloging the dead.

Essentially, Agosín always has been a lyrical love poet in books like *Rain in the Desert*, *Council of the Fairies*, *Toward the Splendid City* and *Starry Night*. Even when her books reclaim family history or critique human rights abuses, they are acts of love. Marjorie Agosín's intuitive vision of poetic transformation discovers value in truths instead of mere facts, creating an ecstatic expression for her authentic spiritual life.

The Old World

El Viejo Mundo

Helena Broder: Angel of Memory

Por la noche son
tan solo tus pasos,
memorias sagradas
de otros tiempos.

Y eran los días
como una fragancia,
la claridad del otoño,
un ruido de pasos
sobre el viento.

        At night,
        only your steps,
        sacred memories
        of other times.

        And the days
        were like a fragrance,
        autumn lightness,
        a sound of steps
        on the wind.

Helena Broder, Vienna, 1939

What should I take to start a new life: photographs of my beloved parents, a book of Goethe's poems? Of course, I will have to leave the keys with the police, the Gestapo, and yet I don't think I shall return. I am leaving for the New World. I am filled with hope. Fate tells me that I should go; that this journey is the beginning of a new life. Have you noticed how perfect Nazi uniforms are? I pity the seamstress who misses a button. It has been very difficult for me to sew this Star of David on my blue coat. But the star is as beautiful as a promise. And yet I must confess that sometimes I cheat the Austrians; I quickly take off my star to go into those stores forbidden to Jews. This is my revenge. Still, I continue to be beautiful and radiant; I love life, garnet rings, and mink stoles. I also love to sing the way my mother taught me, a way to lighten up sorrows. But what should I take? Cooking recipes? I wonder if there will be apples in the New World? My son Joseph is already there, in a port named Valparaíso. They say it is full of beautiful women with naked torsos, and the lights above the hills resemble fireflies.

I am leaving today. Last night I made up my mind, or maybe it was a long time ago. Leaving, fleeing is not foreign to me. I am always ready to pack my bags; this is the destiny of my people. How shall Chile be for us Jews?

Even though the future is becoming undone, and hope is ever so tenuous, I decide to dance. I perfume myself with lilacs, take out my garnet ring, the bracelet Isidor once gave me, and I open my balcony's window. I listen for signs of life, while I remember my mother's face, like that of a full and mischievous moon, radiating light. It is then that I start to move slowly, as if my body responded to the caresses of the wind, and my hands, open palms that know how to love, give and receive, touch the wounds of those Jews forced to clean the sidewalks with acid. My feet, initially resembling small and tender roots, dance as if the world were to end, as if we had arrived at the end of this life. Who could stop dancing? I dance to honor history and memory. My hands are two wings, my feet know all paths, and my voice no longer inhabits a smoke-filled throat.

Light is always present, at the edge of fear, at the edge of history. I have grown accustomed to lighting candles on Friday. Even though I have frequent discussions with God, I still believe in prayer, in the power of prayer as the most clear of miracles, the proof of survival.

My son Mauricio and I have not been able to sleep in several days, hounded by soldiers' boots, the dreadful noise of doors calling the names of those arrested, the decrees dictating who will live, who will die. If I could only remain asleep in the balcony of my house until the war is over, there is so much fear and nightmares. We have no rice, no chicken, nothing to eat; even the birds have prematurely died. And yet, here I am, preparing the trip, full of hope for this new path.

I know that I shall sleep in different countries and learn another language just as you, Joseph, son of mine, had to do upon your arrival in that new land. And yet, I know I will be faithful to my old accent as you were faithful to yours, Josele, my beloved son. But there is eagerness in me, a desire to begin. I am filled with faith and hope.

Yesterday I received a letter from Josele. It had a stamp from Valparaíso with a huge mountain range that reminded me of the Alps. Josele writes sporadically, though he did have a talent for writing love letters; but for me, his mother, it's another story.

I shall wait for the truce. At night it is always the horrific goose-steps, the sound of military boots, with their symmetric and hateful steps, and those carts of death always surrounding the living, picking up the wounded. The nights of Vienna are very strange: nights without fragrances, nights where my memory turns into an abandoned and empty well. Still I cover myself with perfume and read the letter from my son in the New World, here amid a sky full of dreadful scars and omens.

What shall I bring from Vienna, from this house and garden? The world looks like a pile of rubble to me, filled with disjointed doors and windows, lost children and old men. The forced labor camps have been operating for the past two years. We are in the grip of silence and fear. You cannot see the elderly of Vienna. They have crossed borders in the gravity of a savage night, or they have died a few days after their arrival at those infernal camps.

What shall I take for my Josele, the one who left because of love and who will now save our lives, the one who had a very bad temper, but who can now calm me down with his sporadic letters, in the hope of a different life? I know what I shall give him: a bouquet of lilacs from the Pratter. I shall hide leaves inside the feather eiderdown and the fragrance shall be my compass during the crossing of the wild seas of Europe.

It makes me feel safe to leave, not to have to worry about the arrival of my deportation order, or where to spend the night. I have rationally, cautiously thought about who could hide my son Mauricio and me, but truthfully, I don't think there's anyone. The neighbors spit at me when they see me pass by; they close their shutters and call me "Juden." I just smile and think of clouds, perhaps a rainbow or a red poppy. I must hold on to my dreams.

At night a dream keeps recurring; it overflows the evening's horizon. I see fields of red poppies, like dark blood, reassuring us about the persistence of life, the consequences of death, or those unruly poppies, always upright, next to a rusty bicycle in a field of abandoned flowers. I dream with an open-air dance, and the beautiful dresses of women rustling in the wind.

But the question that keeps haunting me is, What to take? It is good to travel light. I will carry a handful of salt to season all the meals and bring good luck to the table, candles for the

Sabbath, china for Passover, and our feather eiderdown under which Isidor and I dreamed of love, made love, and did not speak of the past or the future, but just rejoiced in each other's kisses. That's what I'll take: my eiderdown, the china, and the candelabra to light the way.

All the glass of Vienna's Jews is broken. Last night it was only a giant scream; strident, frozen in fear. I saw how they hurled our elderly neighbors out of balconies. And still I am certain I'll be able to make a beautiful jewel, even out of that broken glass. I shall smooth the edges to fashion a talisman for my trip.

I put on my garnet rings; I am a beautiful woman, a woman alive, full of love. I choose the dress with the lowest cut to seduce the police. I smell of lilacs and violets. I am a garden, an omen of wind. Nothing can stop me from believing in the astonishing power of destiny that today opens in front of me. It is a good sign among the shadows. I close my eyes and see a garden path and imagine love.

Vienna's night is dark and filled with vigilant eyes. Yesterday, Mauricio was forced to clean the sidewalks on his knees. My aunt Loricia is in a staging camp, my aunt Stephania fled to Hungary. I shall never see my cousins again, only in the well of dreams. But today I remember picking up a shard of crystal, and seeing inside it the full possibilities of light.

I have planned everything elegantly and soberly. I cannot be afraid, I will not be afraid because I have faith; I am a woman alone on her way to the New World. I am a worn-out, broken-down island willing to travel. Before I go to the work camp with my deportation order, I hand in the keys at the police. I tell them I am headed for Hamburg.

At night I board a train headed for Hamburg, to catch the ship to Valparaíso. There, in the New Word, Josele is waiting for us. The cards will tell whether I ever return or not. What is essential is to survive; I must overcome the vicissitudes of history. We travel all through the night. I don't think about all my belongings left behind; I am my house, my lighthouse, and my history. Embarking at Hamburg, we sail on a cargo ship from that Europe, slashed with rains and ashes.

My imagination seems blocked, I cannot dream nor sleep, I just hold on to hope, to the power of faith. I left the shadows and ashes with the pyre of burning books. I only imagine that the wind at sea kisses my hair and someone lights the way with a poem.

We sleep on the lower deck. The sea is a sad vault, sometimes it roars, others it is soft like a whisper; in the distance, stars grow smaller and foreign. Most of the time, the refugees sleep on deck, some make love. It is possible to see their faint dance under the covers. One lady has a passionate love affair with a dentist; the next day I find out that he pulls out all of her teeth and replaces them with gold ones. We laugh with the unique joys of love.

Aboard the ship, my son learns to bake pastries. He also falls in love with all the girls on board. I think about Josele and my granddaughter Frida, whom I have only seen in a photograph I brought with me hidden among my feather eiderdown.

War goes on in all its fury. I know that some of my friends have committed suicide; others have answered the call to the camps. More than painful, life is absurd to me. War has made cowards of us all, useless, scared beings. I can't sleep, I dream with Nazi boots, I have nightmares of being decapitated; my chocolate cake is cut open. Life is a bottomless ocean.

We still have two more days of sailing; we approach the coast of Perú. I don't look back; I don't want the specters of memory, only the angels of memory. I love to see the stars; luminous bunches over our eyes. I must learn Spanish. I must learn the names of the stars; the different types of potatoes. This new world is intoxicating in its newfound happiness, and I ask myself how they will greet foreigners in Chile? Shall I be a temporary guest or will I adapt to the sun of this land resembling a rose petal, where volcanoes still roar? How will I be in a different language? Will I be able to translate the darkness hidden within me in bundles of light?

We arrived in South America one dawn, when the Pacific Ocean was a ribbon of sinuous, rose-colored waves like the body of a woman in love. The first thing I saw of this new land was the hills of Valparaíso at dusk, when lights were like dancing fireflies and the savage flowers bent to welcome us into a twilight of unexplored dreams.

Frida will remember with precision the date of your arrival in Chile, in 1939. She will recall the translucent tulle bonnet flowing in the wind, the delicate neckline that insinuated the softness of your neck, still fresh, your delicate breasts, your silver candelabra and the garnet bracelet that has inherited the fate of all our migrations, and now rests peacefully in the hands of your great-granddaughter.

Helena Broder

Se llama
Helena Broder.
Es mi bisabuela
perteneciente
a un linaje de viajeros magos.
Tan solo recuerda
una fecha:
1939,
la noche en Hamburgo
sobre su estola de fuego.
Nunca discutimos el
linaje
ni los objetos transitorios,
la tentación era
olvidar las cenizas
abrazar los espejos
con el rostro encendido de amores.
Eran precarias
nuestras genealogías
grandiosa la memoria.

Helena Broder

Her name is
Helena Broder.
She is my great-grandmother,
belonging to
a line of magician-travelers.
She only remembers
one date:
1939,
the night in Hamburg,
on her stole of fire.
We never discussed
lineage
nor passing things,
the temptation was
to forget the ashes,
to embrace the mirrors,
like ardent lovers.
Our precarious
genealogies
made memory magnificent.

Noche de Viena

En la noche de Viena
acudiste ligera,
como en un sueño de nubes,
a la casa de la vecina,
la que te hablaba de sus geranios,
la que te regalaba el trozo de strudel
y llevaba las llaves de tu casa.

Ella no te reconoció.
Ya eras una judía.
Todo a tu alrededor
era de judía
con olor a judía,
con ropa de judía,
con la muerte de judía.

Dijo que tenía prisa,
que no tenía tiempo para rescatar a otro judío
mientras quemaban en el jardín de geranios.

Viennese Night

One Viennese night
dressed lightly
as a dream of clouds,
you went to your neighbor's house,
the one who talked about her geraniums,
who gave you a slice of strudel,
who kept your house keys.

She did not recognize you.
You were a Jew.
Everything around you
was Jewish:
Jewish smell,
Jewish clothes,
Jewish death.

She said she was in a hurry,
she had no time to rescue another Jew,
while books burned in her garden filled with geraniums.

Maletín de viaje

En un claro
del bosque,
cercano a los precipicios
de la noche cabizbaja
y las ausencias,
ahí estaba
una pequeña maletita
de niña.
Podría haber sido
como la de tu hija,
llena de gracias,
piedras diminutas
y salvajes,
joyas imaginadas.
Podría haber sido la
valija de la novia
con su vestuario de color malva
como el amor
o la lluvia en el alma
después del amor.

Sin embargo,
era la maleta de una
niña judía
la que cantaba de noche
y que vivió tal vez en Praga,
o Amsterdam,
o en una aldea nevada de Rumania.
Su crimen era haber nacido judía
y nada más.

Traveling Bag

In a clearing
of the forest,
close to the edge
of melancholy night
and emptiness,
there lay
a small traveling bag
of a child.
It could have belonged
to your daughter,
full of charms,
wild and tiny pebbles,
imagined jewels.
It could have been
a bride's bag
with her mauve wardrobe
like love
or rain in the soul
after love.

However,
it was the bag
of a Jewish girl,
one who sang at night,
who lived in Prague, perhaps,
or Amsterdam,
or in some snowy Romanian village.
Her crime was to be born Jewish,
nothing more.

De pronto, su maleta se halla
entre las nieblas
y el humo azul,
a la deriva.
No tenía destino
ni dueño y
tan sólo decía
"Auschwitz".

¿Es Auschwitz una ciudad
de muertos o vivos?
preguntó la niña sorprendida.

Era una maletita pequeña
con los tesoros de las niñas
y sus delirios de primavera.
Era una maleta sola,
sin destino y
sin dueño.
Esa maletita fue a dar a
un lugar donde, al llegar,
los niños se llenan
de canas blancas y
ya no miran al cielo.

Más que seguro
en el tiempo del hielo
sin fronteras
algún gendarme nazi
se debió quedar con el botín:
tal vez una muñeca
o un diario,
tal vez semillas de girasol
pero tan sólo un recuerdo.

Suddenly, her bag is found
amid the mist
and blue smoke,
adrift.
It had neither destination
nor owner and
it only said,
"Auschwitz."

Is Auschwitz a city
of the dead or the living?
asked the girl, surprised.

It was a small bag
with the treasures of little girls
and their spring longings,
an abandoned bag,
without destination,
without owner.
This little bag was returned
to a place where,
upon their arrival,
children's hair turned white
and they no longer looked at the sky.

It is more than certain,
in that time of frost
and obliterated borders,
some Nazi soldier
must have kept the loot:
perhaps a doll
or a diary,
maybe sunflower seeds –
no more than a memory.

El impredecible tren del norte

Como un oscurecido viajero,
el conductor del tren
seguro, preciso,
vigila que todos los pasajeros,
inclusive las mujeres calvas,
las vestidas de novia y muerte y
los ancianos jadeantes,
se suban a ese tren
que los llevará
al lugar de la ausencia
más segura,
al lugar de los espantos sin nombre,
al secreto más inexplicable,
el secreto que todos conocemos.

El conductor del tren
es prestigioso en su oficio,
merece una condecoración
por su puntualidad.
Sabe el destino de aquellos trenes:
las estaciones de gas azul,
los parajes de la niebla,
el silencio más allá de todos los silencios,
los cuerpos que arden cuales flores muertas.

El conductor del tren
se considera noble en esa obediencia.
Después de todo
son sólo los judíos que viajan en
esos trenes
y su deber,

Unpredictable Northern Train

Like a darkened traveler,
the train conductor
confident, precise,
checks that all the passengers,
including the shorn women,
those dressed like brides and death,
and the gasping elders,
board this train
that will deliver them
to the place from which
there is no return,
to the place of nameless horrors,
to the most inexplicable secret,
the secret we all know.

The train conductor
is well respected for his work,
deserving of a medal
for his punctuality.
He knows the fate of those trains:
the stations of blue gas,
the home of that fog,
the silence beyond all silences,
where bodies burn like dead flowers.

The train conductor
considers himself noble in this obedience.
After all
it is only Jews who travel
on these trains
and it is his duty,

su vocación apasionada,
es que desaparezcan los judíos.
Antes habían desaparecido los Testigos de Jehová,
las enfermas, las ancianas,
ahora hasta los niños judíos,
un millón y medio para precisar,
deben ir,
y el conductor se alegra
cuando los ve subir,
es muy de noche
aunque es claro ver.
Son bellos y vulnerables,
esos niños,
cadenciosos y ceremoniosos,
con cabelleras luminosas.
Obedecen.
Son sinceros.
Han recorrido el verano sin premura
en esta hora turbia,
siguen siendo buenos
aunque el conductor del tren
detesta a los niños judíos.

El conductor del tren
ama la perfección de la obediencia,
el sonido del tren que se aleja
y se retira,
se aleja y se acerca,
como la niebla que aprisiona.

El conductor del tren
sabe cuándo se abren las puertas de la vida
y de la muerte,
y él sonríe.
Él ama su oficio.

his passionate vocation
to make the Jews disappear.
It was the Jehovah's Witnesses who disappeared first,
then the sick, the old,
now Jewish children,
a million and a half to be precise.
They must go,
and the conductor smiles
watching them board,
it is midnight-dark
but clear enough to see.
They are beautiful and vulnerable
those children,
graceful and ceremonious,
with shinning hair.
They obey.
They are sincere.
They have endured a long, slow summer
in this turbulent time,
yet they seem good
even though the conductor
hates Jewish children.

The train conductor
loves the perfection of obedience,
the sound of the departing train
retreats: recedes and rises,
like the suffocating fog.

The train conductor
knows when the doors of life
and death open,
and he smiles.
He loves his work.

Es noble matar judíos,
ciudadanos de nadie,
niños dementes
deshabitar las palabras del amor y del miedo.

Hoy yo rezo por aquel conductor de tren.
Pido una explicación
por aquellas novias de luto,
por la abuela a quien le sajaron el corazón.
Pido justicia por todos los conductores de tren
que sabían que a ese lugar se llegaba con vida,
y se regresaba con los
compartimentos vacíos,
con algunas muñecas
decapitadas, con libros de hadas
danzando entre la locura.
En esa estación aparecía la muerte,
sin rostro, con tacones translúcidos,
con la lengua jadeante
y el conductor de tren lo sabía.

El conductor de tren
hacía ecos de los silbidos de la muerte.
Insistía en que los trenes tuvieran su
propios calendario,
sus llegadas y partidas.
Amaba los trenes de medianoche
con los niños somnolientos y descalzos,
las madres llorosas, con orejas de pozo triste.

El conductor de tren sonreía
mientras llegaban a Auschwitz
y así terminaba su jornada
heroica.
Había matado a otros judíos.

It is noble to kill Jews,
citizens of nowhere,
demented children
abandoning words of love and fear.

Today I pray for that train conductor.
I demand an explanation
for those brides of mourning,
for the broken-hearted grandmother.
I demand justice for all the train conductors
who knew that they delivered life to that place
and returned with
empty boxcars,
with a few decapitated dolls,
fairy tales
dancing amid madness.
In that station, death appeared
faceless, with translucent heels,
with a panting tongue,
and the train conductor knew.

The train conductor
echoed the whistles of death.
He insisted that trains
run on time,
arriving and departing.
He loved the midnight trains
with sleepy, barefoot children,
weeping mothers with ears like sad wells.

The train conductor smiled
when they arrived at Auschwitz
and his heroic journey
was over.
He had killed more Jews.

Como el color de la niebla

Tus vestidos,
pequeñas embarcaciones de arena
o papel, a la deriva,
donde se calcan los inventos.
Frágiles tus enaguas
sajadas como el ropaje de
las mujeres muertas.
Tus prendas,
tus blusas de encaje color
niebla.
En tu ropa tan
sólo he encontrado
preguntas.

Cuando regresaste a esa casa
de escombros y luz afilada
tu Dios se te hizo cada
vez más ausente
y rezaste por los padres de tus padres muertos.

Te quedaste agazapada en aquel umbral
que antes recibió los gestos de tu niñez,
la felicidad de un lenguaje radiante.
Ahora entras salvaje, sola,
las palabras se quedaron
en tu garganta de humo.

Like the Color of Fog

Your dresses,
tiny boats of sand
or paper, drift
where patterns are traced.
Your fragile petticoats,
ripped like the clothes
of dead women.
Your garments,
your blouses of lace,
the color of fog.
In your belongings
I have found
only questions.

After you returned to that house
of rubble and piercing light,
God grew more difficult to find,
and you prayed
for the parents of your dead parents.

You stayed curled up in that doorway
that had welcomed your childish acts,
the happiness of a radiant language.
Now you enter, feral, alone,
choking on the words
in your smoke-filled throat.

Confesión de los austriacos

Como entre los abismos,
se escuchan las voces
de la disculpa,
¿o serán los rituales adormecidos
del arrepentimiento?
Los austriacos
confiesan pactar
con los colmillos del miedo.
Cabizbajos anuncian un falso desgarro.
Dicen haber robado infancias claras,
arrojado a hombres tras los ventanales,
jugado a ser sepultureros
de los judíos,
de los niños judíos
entre más inocentes
más airados en su ira.

Austrian Confession

As if from the abyss,
complacent voices
make excuses,
or are they the tired rituals
of repentance?
The Austrians
confess their pact
with the fangs of fear.
Heads bowed, they put on a brave show.
Admit to having stolen pure childhoods,
thrown men through windows,
played gravediggers
for the Jews,
for Jewish children.
Toward the most innocent,
their anger was the most perverse.

Girasol herido

I.

Tal vez
fue la
memoria del
instante en que
se negó
el silbido
como aullido,
boca feroz entre los miedos.
Tal vez
fue el estampido,
el color oscuro
devorando la luz
en toda su claridad.
Tal vez
fue lo que
mamá me insinuó
que recuerde.

II.

Gira la memoria como un girasol
herido,
giran las voces, el estampido,
las urdimbres de vidas
de esa noche de cristales rotos.
Recuerdo el estruendo de Dios entre las ausencias,
la niña recostada en su violín
sobre la rajadura de los sueños.

Wounded Sunflower

I.

Maybe
it was the memory
of that instant
in which
the whistling
was held back
like a scream,
ferocious mouth surrounded by fear.
Maybe
it was the loud bang
the dark color
devouring light
in all its clarity.
Maybe
it was what *mamá*
suggested I should
remember.

II.

Memory spins like a wounded
sunflower,
voices turn, the loud bang,
the textures of lives
on that night of broken glass.
I remember the resounding sound of God
among the absences,
the girl lying on her violin upon her broken dreams.

Mi cabeza es un bosque perdido,
un bosque de árboles como raíces, como brazos,
como manos.

III.

A veces por las noches el ruido
estampido en el vacío,
el odio atravesando los cristales,
el odio sobre el rostro de los ancianos,
sobre la niña que toca el violín.
El odio sobre un horizonte entre las nieblas
carcomidas.

IV.

De pronto,
oigo la voz de mi madre
que dice que sí, que
también el cristal roto puede
ser hermoso,
que intentemos hacer de él una crisálida
transparente.

V.

Que recojamos aquellos cristales
de esa noche dantesca
y hagamos de ellos
una historia de luz,
una ráfaga,
una memoria.

Subo las escaleras,
Viena, Berlín,
Madrid, Santiago,

My head is a lost forest,
a forest with trees like roots, like arms,
like hands.

III.

Sometimes at night, the noise
thunders in the emptiness,
hatred penetrating the glass,
hatred on the face of the elderly,
on the girl playing the violin.
Hatred on the horizon, among
the consumed fog.

IV.

Suddenly,
I hear my mother's voice
saying that yes,
broken glass can also
be beautiful,
that we should try to turn it into a transparent
cocoon.

V.

We should gather those pieces of glass
from that horrific night
and make out of them
a story of light,
a gust of wind,
a memory.

I climb the stairs,
Vienna, Berlin,
Madrid, Santiago,

y cuelgo esos cristales de
mi balcón
para que lleguen palomas extraviadas,
ángeles generosos y terrenales.
Que estos pedazos de vidrio
no nos corten el corazón ni el habla,
que no sean memoriales de niebla
y olvidos como los cuerpos
deshechos.

Y esa noche como ninguna otra,
cuando todo tenía olor a miedo, a rapto, a delirio,
mi madre me dijo que podríamos recoger
los cristales rotos
y hacer de ellos un arcoiris de luz.

and I hang the glass from
my balcony
for the arrival of lost doves,
generous and earthly angels,
so that these fragments of glass
cut neither heart nor voice,
so as not to become memorials of fog
and oblivion, like destroyed
bodies.

And that night unlike any other night
when everything smelled of fear, of abduction,
of madness,
my mother told me that we could gather
the broken glass
and turn it into a rainbow.

Sobre Terezin, Helena Broder solloza

Dicen que el viento
amordazado no levantaba las hojas
ni los cuerpos de aquellos niños,
espectros de vida,
presagios de la muerte.

Dicen que habían levantado muros
y vigilantes.
Los niños no llevaban lápices
bajo el brazo,
tan sólo estrellas amarillas:
estrellas ajustadas a los brazos
de aquellos niños
sin delitos,
sin grandes ni pequeños crímenes.
Eran niños, tan sólo,
con sus estrellas doradas
y sus trajes oscuros
para agregar más sombra
a ese lugar entre las lejanías
a ese tiempo sin tiempo,
a esos vientos sin viento.

Y los niños aprendieron
a seguir el
aliento de la marcha de
las cosas.
Vieron la luz de Dios
entre los alambres.

Helena Broder Sobs over Terezin

They say the wind was muzzled,
unable to lift the leaves
nor the bodies of those children,
specters of life,
portents of death.

They say they had raised
walls, placed watchmen.
The children had no pencils
under their arms,
only yellow stars:
stars sewn to the sleeves
of those children
without offences,
without crimes, big or small.
They were children, only children,
with their golden stars
and their dark suits
that only deepened the shadows
in that remote place,
in that timeless time,
among breathless winds.

And the children learned
to follow
the breath of the movement
of things.
They saw the light of God
on the barbed wire.

Algunos dibujaron mariposas
vivas y muertas.
Otros las vocaciones del viento.

Dicen que era un lugar
donde el silencio se erizaba
por las noches;
donde el olvido
era un soberano
tras el lenguaje de
las alambradas
donde Dios permaneció
en los corredores muertos de la fe.

Some drew butterflies,
alive and dead,
others, the doings of the wind.

They say it was a place
where silence bristled
through the night;
where oblivion
reigned
behind the language
of barbed wire
where God resided
in the deathly corridors
of faith.

Primas

Mi madre murmuraba
al nombrarlas,
Julia, Silvia, Sonia,
Sonia, Julia, Silvia.
Eran nombres de ríos,
nombres de mujeres hadas.
Eran mis primas,
mujeres conocidas,
con las que compartíamos una historia.
Yo las amaba desde lejos
y desde cerca.

No sabíamos nada de ellas.
Poco se sabía del tiempo obstinado de la guerra,
tan sólo ciertas claves,
un murmullo
como un suspiro.
Nos enviaban direcciones secretas,
jamás resueltas,
pistas falsas,
nombres invisibles.

Para las fiestas sagradas
había puestos vacíos
y mi padre, con su copa sagrada,
las nombraba,
Julia, Sonia, Silvia.

Cousins

My mother murmurs
as she names them,
Julia, Silvia, Sonia
Sonia, Julia, Silvia.
They were the names of rivers,
the names of fairy women.
They were my cousins,
women we knew,
with whom we shared a history.
I loved them from a distance,
and I loved them intimately.

We knew nothing about them.
Little was known about those grim war years,
only certain clues,
a whisper,
like a sigh.
They sent us addresses in code,
never deciphered,
false trails,
invisible names.

On holy days
their seats were vacant
and my father, with his sacred cup,
invoked their names:
Julia, Sonia, Silvia.

Yo llegué también a quererlas.
Me conformaba con
conocer sus letras
en raídas postales
de Viena, luego
Praga y
luego las ciudades de nombres austeros.

Mi abuela Helena,
taciturna
sacaba sus fotografías que
parecían huesos color de ámbar,
brillando entre las ausencias.
De pronto,
casi cincuenta años
después,
llama el primo de Suecia,
y no puede dejar de recordar.

Nos contó,
mudo,
delgado entre la distancia,
que las había visto,
a esas primas:
Julia, Sonia, Silvia.
Las había encontrado
en el libro sagrado de
los muertos.
Las había buscado por
sus apellidos,
y sus travesías.

I too came to love them,
was comforted to see
their handwriting
on frayed postcards
from Vienna, then
Prague, and later still,
the cities with austere names.

My grandmother Helena,
taciturn,
took out her photographs that
resembled amber-colored bones,
bright among the absences.
Then out of the blue,
almost fifty years later,
the cousin from Sweden calls
and he cannot help but remember.

He told us,
mute,
ethereal at that distance,
that he had seen them,
those cousins:
Julia, Sonia, Silvia.
He had found them
in the sacred book
of the dead.
He had searched
for their last names,
and their transfers.

Habían sido trasladadas en aquellos
trenes de sombras
y calvas mujeres
cantando con sus trajes azules
a Terezin
para luego mandarlas a
Auschwitz
donde no hay olvidos,
donde no hay calendarios,
donde no hay memoria,
donde no hay voz,
donde las mujeres enmudecen,
son rapadas,
deliran
y hacen de sus cabezas los ceremoniales
de los pájaros muertos.

El primo de Suecia
las encontró.
Estaban muertas y vivas
o habían llegado en una tarde de ámbar
heridas y muertas.

Me dice rápidamente
que las mataron con el gas azul
y que eso es todo lo que se sabe de ellas.
Dice que se lo cuente a mi madre
y a la madre de mi madre,
también a la tía Regina.

Todas ellas
en Auschwitz
y yo no sé cómo nombrarlas
y no sé cómo recordarlas.

They had been sent
to those trains full of shadows
and shorn women,
singing in their blue clothes,
bound for Terezin,
later sent on to
Auschwitz,
where there is no forgetting,
where there are no calendars,
where there is no memory,
where there is no voice,
where women keep silent,
are shorn.
They are delirious
and carry in their heads the rites
of dead birds.

The cousin from Sweden
found them.
They were both dead and alive,
or they had arrived one amber afternoon,
wounded and dead.

He tells me hurriedly
that they were killed with blue gas
and that this is all he knows of them.
He asks me to tell this to my mother,
and also to Aunt Regina.

All of them
in Auschwitz,
and I don't know how to name them,
and I don't know how to remember them.

La ira se confunde con mi aullido.
Las reconozco
Sonia, Julia, Silvia.
Ya no puedo nombrarlas
y las veo sajadas en esos bosques
de mariposas muertas
y pienso que no merezco esta vida
sin ellas.

Le digo a mi madre
y a mi abuela, que ha quedado
olvidada en el sur,
que no
debemos buscarlas.
Que no estipulemos falsos
presagios;
que ahí están;
que al llegar
las hicieron arder;
que sus huesitos fueron colocados
sin nombre en los hornos diminutos
de la muerte.

Me nublo toda al contarte esta historia
y sólo la cuento en un poema
porque no puedo decírsela a nadie.
No quiero oír cosas como
"Otra vez los judíos y sus memorias".
"Eso pasó hace años".
"Yo no sé nada del asunto".
Así hablaban cuando se desapareció el vecino,
el abuelo,
sus nietos pequeños.

Fury blends with my screams.
I recognize them
Sonia, Julia, Silvia.
I am unable to name them anymore,
I see them mutilated in those forests
of dead butterflies
and I think: I do not deserve this life
without them.

I tell my mother
and my grandmother, who remained
forgotten in the South,
that we should not
search for them.
That there is no need to pursue
false leads;
that they are there;
that they were incinerated
as soon as they arrived;
their tiny bones were laid
nameless in the little ovens
of death.

Telling you this story
distresses me,
I can only say it in a poem
as I am unable to tell it to anyone.
I don't want to hear things like:
"Again, the Jews and their memories."
"That happened years ago."
"I don't know anything about that."
That is how they talked when
the neighbor, the grandfather,
and his small grandchildren were abducted.

Esta noche
gira y gira en mi cabeza
como un atado de amapolas
muertas.
Ya sé dónde están Julia, Sonia, Silvia.
Iré a navegar esos prados.
Mi pasión besará esos céspedes
esperando encontrar sus labios.

Julia, Sonia, Silvia,
no morirán entre los alambres.
No serán más los judíos ocultos
sin cabellos y sin lenguaje.

Yo regresaré a los campos
para regarlos con rezos y agua santa
te regalaré un cuaderno, Julia,
un abanico, Sonia,
un soplo de luz, Silvia.
Primas mías, primas hermanas mías,
familia que nunca llegó a ser amada más.
No quiero engaños para vuestros nombres.
No quiero que nadie hable
por vuestros nombres.
Pido un segundo, un siglo de paz
y memoria
para todas
las judías muertas,
las gitanas,
las mujeres de Bosnia.
Todas se llaman
Julia, Silvia, Sonia
y son mías.
Se sientan para las fiestas sagradas,
y antes de brindar
las nombramos.

Like a bouquet
of wilted poppies,
this night
keeps turning in my head.

I don't know where they are: Julia, Sonia, Silvia.
I shall navigate those meadows.
In my passion I will kiss the grass
hoping to encounter their lips.

Julia, Sonia, Silvia,
you shall not die tangled in barbed wire.
You will no longer be hidden Jews
without hair, without a voice.

I will return to the fields
to sprinkle them with prayers and holy water.
I shall give you a notebook, Julia,
a fan, Sonia,
a breath of light, Silvia.
My cousins, my blood cousins,
family members I will never embrace.
I don't want lies for your names.
I don't want anybody to speak
on your behalf.
I ask for a second, for a century of peace
and memory
for every single one:
the dead Jews,
the gypsies,
the women of Bosnia.
They are all named
Julia, Silvia, Sonia
and they all are mine.

Los ángeles inclinados de Helena Broder

De pronto soñaste
que los umbrales de casa
eran ángeles inclinados.
Comenzaste a nombrarlos
a cada uno de ellos
en voz alta
rápida.
Era como tus hermanas,
cálidas y transparentes,
brisas malvas en un día de fiesta.

De pronto soñaste
que tal vez estaban ahí,
junto a tu memoria
en este paisaje de jazmines
y azahares;
este paisaje que no huele
a carnes muertas.

Entonces soñaste
que esas, tus hermanas,
eran ángeles y que te decían
"Buenos días, Helena Broder".
Yo me puse también a silbar sus nombre
y tu mano fue como el dibujo del viento
sobre la mano de Dios.

The Leaning Angels of Helena Broder

Suddenly, you dreamt that
the lintels of your house
were leaning angels.
You began to name
each one of them
in a voice high
and fast.
They were like your sisters:
warm and transparent,
mauve breezes on a festive day.

Suddenly, you dreamt
that perhaps they were there,
next to your memory
in this landscape of jasmines
and orange blossoms;
this landscape devoid of the stench
of dead flesh.

Then you dreamt
that these, your sisters,
were angels who said to you,
"Good morning, Helena Broder."
I too began to whistle their names
and your hand was like a sketch of wind
upon the hand of God.

Llegas a Praga

Has llegado a Praga,
buscas tu memoria en
los sueños,
se precipitan tus recuerdos,
los ancestros muertos
reprochan tu regreso,
los duendes y los dibuks
a tu alrededor tienen risas
maléficas.
Pero eres obstinado,
eliges el regreso,
vivir entre los fantasmas,
oír sus voces,
verlos en la plaza
dispuestos, obedientes
para abordar el tren
que los llevará al famélico
horror de un sueño.

Has regresado para vivir en ellos,
despedirte de sus jardines,
perdonar sus orgullos y los tuyos.

Te detienes en una sinagoga que
guarda maletines de viaje de
niñas muertas en primavera.
En los sueños las amas,
tus manos hacen de sus cabellos
guirnaldas,
ellas viven en tu sueño,
en tu labio que besa y nombra.

Arrival in Prague

You have arrived in Prague,
searching your memory
in dreams,
your thoughts rushing.
Dead ancestors
reproach your return,
while spirits and dibuks
laugh malevolently
around you.
But you are obstinate,
you choose to return,
to live among ghosts,
hearing their voices,
watching them
willing and obedient in the square,
ready to board the train
that will take them to the starved
horror of a dream.

You have returned to live among them,
to leave behind their gardens,
forgive their pride and yours.

You stop at a synagogue that
holds traveling bags from
those girls who died in spring.
In your dreams you love them,
your hands make garlands
with their hair,
they live in your dreams,
on your lips that kiss and name them.

Regresas temerosa.
También tú has llegado a Hades,
has deseado estar con Persépone.
Pero en Praga
despiertas,
tu voz se llena de nombres,
tu voz es una caricia,
un violín encontrado entre los sótanos
y los arreboles.

Alguien vigila tus pasos,
te enseña el camino que
más que sendero es ilusión.
Tu mirada se vuelve musgo
y en las noches miras las cúpulas
asediadas por la magia y la demencia.
Crees en el amor, en la irracionalidad del odio.

Por fin
puedes llorar,
el corazón liviano,
como umbral,
como un vaivén
de pájaros.
Regresas de esa noche de olvido y memoria,
el ángel de la historia
te cubre de promesas.

En tus ojos, los ojos
de esas niñas muertas.

El ángel de la memoria
es tu promesa.

Fearful, you return.
You have also arrived at Hades,
have wished to be with Persephone.
But in Prague you
wake up,
your voice is filled with names,
it is a caress,
a violin found among cellars and
reddish clouds.

Someone watches your steps,
showing you the way that
more than a path is an illusion.
Your gaze turns to moss
and at night you gaze at cupolas
besieged by magic and madness.
You believe in love, in the irrationality of hate.

At last
you can cry,
your heart is light
like a threshold,
a movement
of birds.
You return from that night of oblivion and memory,
the angel of history
covers you with promises.

In your eyes, the eyes
of those dead girls.

The angel of memory
is your promise.

Tus pasos sobre la nieve de Praga

Ningún lenguaje
canta tus pasos sobre
la nieve de Praga,
ni tus manos sobre aquellas estatuas
en el puente Carlos que al
verte pasar hacen pequeñas reverencias
y celebran tu asombro.

Aún no llevas la estrella
de David
en tu ojal oscurecido.
Aún caminas, te deslizas,
te resbalas
y eres una niña en las
calles de Praga
sobre la nieve austera,
te bendicen
sus relojes de magos inquietos y
su cúpula de cielo fosforescente.

Ningún lenguaje
canta tus pasos
sobre la nieve de Praga.
Piensas que todos somos hermanos.
Tu estrella dorada reluce febril
sobre la nieve que protege tus pasos.
No la escondes.
La luces orgullosa.
Te alumbra mientras las
estatuas cambian de rostro,
la oración de la noche es
un canto de ausencias.

Your Footsteps in the Snow of Prague

No song tells
of your footsteps
in the snow of Prague,
or of your hands on those statues
on King Charles Bridge
that make small curtsies as you pass
and laugh at your astonishment.

Still, you do not carry
the Star of David
in your dark buttonhole.
Still, you walk, you glide,
you slip,
you are a girl in
the streets of Prague
on the austere snow,
blessed by the clocks
of restless magicians and
its cupola of phosphorescent sky.

No song tells
of your footsteps
in the snow of Prague.
You think we are all brothers.
Your golden star shines feverishly
on the snow that protects your passing.
You do not hide it.
It shines proudly.
You are illuminated
as the statues change their faces,
the night's prayer is
a song of absences.

El gólem de Praga

Como si camináramos sobre el agua,
las estatuas parecen llorar
y tú lloras con ellas.
Recuerdas a Helena Broder,
paseándose antes del sábado
cuando llegan las primeras
estrellas y la premura del atardecer.
La noche del sábado llega con su aletargada
y clarividente luz.

Caminos trastornados y sordos,
sé que vivimos en la memoria,
o en la metáfora de la memoria,
o en la memoria que no deja olvidos,
que no permite promesas,
o en la imaginación de una memoria
que juega con la distancia,
es un pequeño cascabel que suena
sombrío sobre el reino de los muertos.

En Praga
donde vivieron los primos
que hoy veo vivos,
vivos de verdad y no en el sueño de la muerte que
atraviesa mis pasos y los murmullos de la vigilia.
Están aquí.
Nos esperaban.

Iremos a la casa de Kafka
donde vivía desdoblado y solo
junto a otros judíos solos y desdoblados.

The Golem of Prague

As if we had been walking on water,
the statues appear to cry
and you cry with them.
You remember Helena Broder,
strolling the day before Saturday,
when the first stars arrived
and night fell so rapidly.
Saturday night arrives with its lethargic
clairvoyant light.

The paths ahead are confused, mute.
I know that we live in memory,
or in the metaphor of memory,
or in a memory that allows neither oblivion
nor promises,
or in the imagination of a memory
that plays with distance,
a small somber bell sounding
upon the kingdom of the dead.

In Prague lived the cousins
whom I see today, alive for the first time,
truly alive, not merely in the dream of death
that crosses my steps, murmuring as I watch
through the night.
They are here.
They were waiting for us.

We will go to Kafka's house
where he lived openly and alone
united with other Jews, alone and unhidden.

Los turistas del Holocausto
leen a Kafka en el cementerio de los muertos arrimados
y ya no sé si estamos cruzando aguas
turbias o es la lluvia sobre las
tardes de Praga.

No sé si van a nuestro encuentro los gólems
o son tus pasos, Helena Broder, toda vestida
de ámbar con granates,
con un anillo rojizo en tus manos claras.
Tu caminar es como la plenitud
de la felicidad clandestina.
Repites rezos
y cadencias leves sobre las estatuas.
Llueve esta tarde en toda Europa
y sobre toda la ciudad de Praga.
Nos apresuramos porque llegará el sábado
y los muertos repetirán a los vivos
sus truculentas ofrendas.
Estás tú ahí, toda vestida de muerta,
toda hechizada y fantasmagórica.

Llueve sobre las estatuas de Praga.
Alguien nos toca el hombro
y aligeramos el paso.

Alguien escribió sobre los puentes:
había una ciudad fantasma
y el gólem de Praga
presidía sobre ella.

The tourists of the Holocaust
read Kafka in the cemetery of the discarded dead,
and I no longer know if we are crossing troubled waters
or if it is the afternoon rain of Prague.

I don't know if it is Golems who have come to meet us
or if it is your footsteps, Helena Broder, all dressed up
in amber and garnets,
with a red ring in your clear hands.
Your walk is like the consummation
of some clandestine joy.
You recite prayers
and light verses by the statues.
This afternoon it rains
throughout Europe
and all over the city of Prague.
We hurry because Saturday is coming
and the dead will repeat
their gruesome offerings to the living.
There you are, in the garments of death,
bewitched and phantasmagoric.

It rains on the statues of Prague.
Somebody touches a shoulder
and we quicken our pace.

Somebody wrote of the bridges:
there was a ghost town
and the Golem of Prague
presided over it.

Rue de Rosier

Para John

Como en los pasos
lentos y encantados
del amor,
bajo un cielo de estrellas que rezan,
cruzamos la rue de Rosier
y en voz baja oímos a los judíos
cantar o rezar.
Oíamos murmullos de pájaros
y cortejos de nombres.

Te dije:
"Son los judíos que rezan
en la rue de Rosier".
Pero tú no los oías.
Las palabras como cantos y gemidos
te eran ajenas.
Yo las aprendí
de los secretos
de familia,
como las recetas escogidas
y los pactos ambiguos.
Yo reconocía
a esos invisibles judíos de la rue de Rosier,
quemados en las hogueras blancas
donde oficiaban los sacerdotes sus
imperdonables ceremonias.
Los llevaban y cercaban
en los campos sin hierba,
en los campos sin fragancia de jazmines.

Rue de Rosier

For John

As with the deliberate and
enchanted steps
of love,
we crossed the rue de Rosier
beneath chanting stars
and heard the hushed voices
of Jews singing,
praying,
listened to the cooing of birds
and processions of names.

I told you:
"Those are the Jews praying
on the Rue de Rosier."
But you couldn't hear them.
The words, like songs and lamentations,
were foreign to you.
I learned them
from family secrets,
like favorite recipes
and illicit affairs.
I recognized
those invisible Jews of the Rue the Rosier,
burned in the white pyres
where priests conducted
unforgivable ceremonies.
They captured them, surrounded them
in barren fields,
in meadows without the fragrance of jasmine.

Los reconocí
a los judíos de la rue de Rosier.
Me golpeaban el hombro.
Me regalaban bosques y niñas perdidas
sujetando candelabros de siete velas.

Tú y yo,
enamorados,
caminando por la rue de Rosier.
Tu mano se aferra y contempla la mía.
Yo sólo escucho el paso de los judíos de la rue de Rosier
centelleando con sus estrellas doradas.

I recognized
the Jews of the Rue de Rosier.
They tapped at my shoulder,
offered me forests and missing girls
clutching candelabras with seven candles.

You and I,
in love,
walking down the Rue de Rosier.
Your hand grasps mine as if in wonder.
I only hear the soft footsteps
of the Jews along the Rue de Rosier
glimmering with their golden stars.

Huellas

para Paul Nakazawa

Más que una memoria
o el sitial donde la memoria
reside como textura,
más que una presencia
entre los fantasmas y los duendes centellantes,
entre las llamas,
en ese lugar de pozo movedizo,
encontré huellas,
tan solo huellas,
despojos, sílabas náufragas,
alfabetos calvos.

Trozos de memoria,
indicios y ángeles mudos.
Trozos giratorios, un extravío, un murmullo,
huellas.

Más que la memoria,
las huellas de portones incendiados,
de calles, de ciudades,
tan solo huellas,
huellas sublimes,
de lo vanamente humillado,
huellas de los pasos heridos,
huellas de los maletines y el alma saqueados.
Huellas de un maletín azul.

Más que la memoria,
y la huella de esa memoria.

Traces

for Paul Nakazawa

More than a memory,
or the place where memory lives,
like a texture,
more than a presence,
among the phantoms and flickering spirits,
in the wandering heart of night,
among the flames
in that unsettled place,
I found traces,
only traces,
cast-off, shipwrecked syllables,
shattered alphabets.

Fragments of memory,
vestiges and mute angels.
Fragments, spinning, wandering, murmuring,
traces.

More than a memory,
traces of fiery portals,
of streets, of cities,
only traces,
sublime traces
of meaningless humiliation,
traces of wounded steps,
traces of pillaged suitcases and plundered souls,
traces of a blue suitcase.

More than a memory,
in the vestiges of that memory,

sentí una voz
que exigía el sagrado silencio
el silencio de la poesía,
el decoro de la poesía.

Tan solo una voz
sumergida,
una voz que su oficio
era solo el recuerdo,
la tenacidad persistente
del recuerdo.

Y en esa voz,
más allá de la zona frágil,
de la memoria
y la crueldad del silencio,
se convocaron los muertos y los vivos,
con sus pasos ágiles alrededor de las tumbas
y los vivos se deslizan como danzarines sabios
sobre estas tumbas de ciudades muertas
y nefastas.

En el transcurso de aquellas caminatas
repiten nombres que son el filo más helado del lenguaje:
Auschwitz, Dacha,
Treblinka.
"El trabajo los hará libres".

Y en esos nombres,
la huella,
el presagio, el indicio, el párpado incendiado
y en esa huella una civilización erradicada
en el más perverso de los escándalos.

I sensed a voice
that demanded sacred silence,
the silence of poetry,
the gravity of poetry.

Only a voice,
submerged,
a voice whose only purpose
was to remember,
the persistent tenacity
of remembrance.

And in this voice,
beyond the fragile bounds of memory,
and the cruelty of silence,
the dead and the living convened,
to dance around tombs,
and the living moved deftly, like wise dancers,
over those graves of dead
and dreadful cities.

In the midst of those walks,
they repeated names from the frozen edge of language:
Auschwitz, Dachau,
Treblinka.
"Work will make you free."

And in those names,
the trace,
the omen, the sign of the burning eyelid,
and in that trace, an obliterated civilization
in the most perverse of scandals.

Aquí, en Yad Vashem
fíjense en el millón de huellas que vamos dejando
en estas grutas de la muerte,
en estos jardines de la muerte.

Más que la paz,
aquí, en Yad Vashem
se exige, se deslumbra, se llama al recuerdo,
al gesto del recuerdo,
a la luz de la memoria
que es una sola voz,
un solo caminar entre los alambres
de las púas
y el bosque de rosas claras.

Humilde se llega a Yad Vashem,
el silencio es un regocijo, una paz,
una estrella,
el silencio es el de los abismos y los precipicios.
Alguien enciende una llama
alguien recoge una flor,
se dejan huellas, testamentos lúcidos
de la historia.
Alguien camina entre los escombros
y se escucha un lamento,
una cadencia,
huellas,
un nombre,
un pueblo que gime,
un pueblo que ora
y resplandece.

Here in Yad Vashem
look at the million traces we have left behind
in these grottos of death,
in these gardens of death.

More than peace,
here in Yad Vashem
they demand, they glare, they cry out for remembrance,
for the gesture of remembrance,
for the light of memory
that is one voice,
a solitary walk among the barbed wire
and forests of pale roses.

Humble, arriving at Yad Vashem,
silence is gladness, peace,
a star,
the stillness of the abyss and the precipice.
Someone lights a flame,
someone picks a flower,
they leave traces,
lucid testaments of history.
Someone walks among the rubble
and listens to a lament,
a cadence,
traces,
a name,
a people who cry out,
a people who pray
and are
resplendant.

The New World

El Nuevo Mundo

1939

Supo ella seducir al destino,
vaticinar la hora de la huida
en 1939, vestida con el traje
de noche y la dicha
en los umbrales del agrio
puerto de Hamburgo.
Navegó,
resuelta a la vida,
hasta los mares del sur.

1939

She knew how to deceive her destiny,
how to predict the right moment to flee
in 1939, dressed as if
for an evening party,
even on the frightening docks
of the port of Hamburg.
Resolved to live,
she set sail
for the southern seas.

Chile, 1939

I.

Como si tu elegancia fuese aquella
de las damas viajadas,
mujeres con el cabello liso y tomado
en un broche de granate,
o una trenza como diadema
elevando el rostro,
como si tus manos no fuesen tatuadas,
tan sólo fuentes claras donde
el agua danza delgada sobre ellas,
cubiertas por las nobles alhajas de familia,
te paseas por el hemisferio sur,
transparente con tus sedas de marfil
tu sombrero de tul violeta
y es paciente tu andar.

II.

Sorprendidos te miran los señores
como si fueras
una turista extravagante
o la anciana del barrio o la loca
con el color violeta.
Pocos saben lo que ocultas
tu rostro borrado por las sombras,
tu soledad como un cofre sellado.
Pocos saben de tus brazos
siempre abiertos
ni las ceremonias de la demencia
todas las noches.

Chile, 1939

I.

With your elegance like that
of well-traveled ladies,
with their silky hair
pinned by a garnet brooch,
or braided like a diadem
crowning the face,
as if your hands were not tattooed,
but only clear sources
where water dances lightly over them,
covered by noble family jewels,
you stroll across the southern hemisphere,
transparent in your ivory-colored silks,
your bonnet of violet tulle
and your patient walk.

II.

Astonished, men look at you,
as if you were an extravagant tourist,
or the neighborhood's eldest matron
or some local madwoman
turning violet.
Few know what you hide,
your face erased by shadows,
your loneliness like a sealed chest;
few know of your arms,
ever open,
or your nightly rites
of madness.

III.

Caminas por las avenidas pobladas
de gomeros,
de vendedores de higos y frutas frescas.
De pronto en el sol fulgurante te detienes
como si en aquel herido corazón
las palabras surgieran en un latir
y comienzas a decir:
"Una vez en Viena . . .
una vez en Viena"
y llegan a tus pies
los ángeles de la memoria.

III.

You walk by the solemn avenues
inhabited by rubber trees,
and the merchants
with their figs and fresh fruit.
Suddenly, you pause beneath the blazing sun
as if your wounded heart
were pulsing words,
and you begin to say:
"Once in Vienna . . .
once in Vienna"
and the angels of memory
arrive at your feet.

Creí que eras un ángel, Helena

Creí que eras un
ángel
a tientas por los
corredores,
una huésped
extraña a
tus propias pertenencias.

Creí que eras un ángel
que reza mientras atraviesa
corredores vacíos,
vidas perplejas y cantos como rezos cálidos.
Pero eras tú, abuela mía,
vagando por la noche
por tu casa de la memoria,
escribiendo palabras que se deslizan
en el silencio
que desvaría ajena tras los cuartos quebrados.
¿A quién buscabas tan leve y pequeña
con tu camisón blanco
y una linterna de menudos?

Creí que eras un ángel
y jugué a descubrir cada uno
de tus mensajes,
mensajera de la vida breve,
de la memoria frágil,
jardinera de flores nocturnas.

I Thought you Were an Angel, Helena

I thought you were
an angel
sensing your way
along the corridors,
a stranger
among your own
belongings.

I thought you were an angel,
praying, while walking
through empty hallways,
perplexed lives and songs like soft prayers.
It was you, my grandmother,
wandering at night,
through your house of memory,
writing words that glide
into silence,
delirious, facing shattered rooms.
Who were you looking for, so light and small,
in your white nightgown,
with your tiny lantern?

I thought you were an angel
and I played at discovering
each one of your messages,
messenger of intense life,
of the frail memory,
a gardener of nocturnal flowers.

Helena sueña con el viento

Más allá de los regresos
y las huellas
de un caminar errado
fui recogida por el viento
reconocida ante sus caricias.

Danzando tras los umbrales
el viento me descubre
sin secretos
plenos y solos
ante el signo de sus murmullos.

Ven,
me dijo
el viento
sobre el árbol,
y yo acudí
ante esa llamada
como una memoria
sagrada.

Helena Dreams of the Wind

Beyond the returns
and the footsteps
of a misguided walk
I was lifted by the wind,
recognized by its caresses.

Dancing in the doorway,
the wind finds me
without secrets,
complete and alone,
before the sign of its murmurs.

Come,
the wind
told me
from above the tree,
and I answered
that call
like a sacred
memory.

El cuaderno de direcciones de Helena

Has guardado tus pertenencias,
la blusa de encaje lila
que hace juego con tu cabello
de hada sabia y antigua.
Has preparado tu valija
 y el cuaderno de direcciones
está en tu brazo.
¿A quién buscas, Helena Broder,
después de la guerra?
¿A quién encontrarás en esas direcciones
dobladas,
en esas casas que no se encuentran?
¿Qué pasos danzaron por
tu jardín?
¿Qué vecino te delató
mientras podabas las rosas?
¿Quién habrá regado tus geranios?
¿Adónde vas
Helena Broder
después de la lluvia
y la desierta puerta de las guerras?
Un viento negro te cobija.
Voces mudas te aguardan.
El cuaderno de direcciones arde.

Helena's Address Book

You have put away your belongings,
the lacey lilac blouse
that matches your hair
like that of some wise and ancient fairy.
You have prepared your suitcase
and the address book
is in your arms.
Who are you searching for, Helena Broder,
after the war?
Who will you find in those
folded addresses,
in those houses that you cannot find?
What steps danced in
your garden?
What neighbor gave you away
while you trimmed the roses?
Who may have watered your geraniums?
Where are you going,
Helena Broder,
after the rain
and the deserted door of the wars?
A black wind protects you.
Mute voices await you.
The address book is burning.

Los sueños de Helena Broder

¿Abuela, por qué sueñas con mujeres rapadas?
¿Quién oye tu voz mientras rezas el rezo
de la noche y reposa el desierto de la noche
sobre tu cabellera de humo?

Hoy llueve sobre el sur de Chile.
Aprendes a nombrar los pájaros,
los cerros de campos despoblados.
Viena es lejana en tu memoria.
Has dejando atrás tus palabras
en los bosques de cenizas.

The Dreams of Helena Broder

Grandmother, why do you dream of shorn women?
Who hears your voice when you pray the evening prayer
and the desert night falls
on your hair of smoke?

Today it rains throughout southern Chile.
You learn to name the birds,
the hills of deserted fields.
Vienna is a far away memory.
You have left your words behind
in the forests of ashes.

Helena Broder contempla el cielo

I.

Mirando el cielo
supe entonar las fugitivas palabras
de la noche.

II.

Todo claro
y luminoso,
el cielo como un racimo
entre las estrellas.

III.

Era una ciudad imaginaria,
el cielo
donde anidaban los nombres
de los muertos y los vivos.

IV.

De todas las ocupaciones
ella cultivó el arte de mirar
al cielo,
supo reconocer las estrellas
como quien reconoce el paso del amor.

Helena Broder Contemplates the Sky

I.

Looking at the sky
I learned to sing the fugitive words
of night.

II.

Everything clear
and bright,
the sky clustered
with stars.

III.

It was an imaginary city,
the sky,
where nested the names
of the dead and the living.

IV.

Of all the occupations,
she cultivated the art of looking
at the sky,
she learned to recognize the stars
as someone who recognizes the passing of love.

V.

Por las noches,
cuando la luz del viento
era un pequeño canasto de fuegos,
inclino mi cuerpo
sobre la tierra,
elevo con suavidad
la vista
al cielo,
un estrella dorada
sobre la esperanza.

V.

At night,
when the light of the wind
is a small basket of fire,
I recline my body
on the earth,
gently, I look
skyward,
a golden star
of hope.

Diminutos son tus pies, Helena

Te escucho deambular por el
cuarto como quien
pisa el abismo de los sueños,
sonámbula y
descalza por las maderas
de esta tierra del sur.
Diminutos son tus pies, Helena Broder,
gigante tu estrella
y milagrosa tu salvación.

Escucho tras las noches eléctricas
tus gestos.
Estás a salvo abuela, te digo.
Me susurras en el oído
rezos, cantos en el idioma del enemigo
y lloras a borbotones
mientras me dices
"*Meine liebe, meine liebe*".
Yo digo el Ave María en
el idioma de los indios.
No lo reconoces.
Pero cantas como en un rezo.

Como una testigo muda
aprendo tu idioma
me inclino sobre las palabras que has tocado
al igual que mi madre
que cepilla tu cabellos,
que urde trenzas y cenizas.

Your Feet Are Tiny, Helena

I hear you walking
across the room like someone
tiptoeing over an abyss of dreams,
sleepwalking with bare feet
on the wooden floors
of this southern land.
Your feet are tiny, Helena Broder,
but your star is gigantic,
your survival miraculous.

I hear your movements
in the electric nights.
You are safe grandmother, I tell you.
You whisper in my ear
prayers, songs in the enemy's language
and you cry waterfalls
while you say
"*Meine liebe, meine liebe*".
I say a Hail Mary in an
Indian language.
You do not recognize it,
but chant as if praying.

Like a mute witness,
I learn your language,
I lean over the words you have touched,
just like my mother
who brushes your hair,
who mixes braids and ashes.

Helena Broder conmemora el blanco y negro

Todavía ella se acerca,
murmura, suspira
por ese rostro,
por esa fotografía
que ha estado muerta
por más de tres décadas.
Ya no busca
en la oscuridad ahuecada
de las ciudades,
ya no va a la plaza.

Tan solo se acerca
sobre esta fotografía
y le dice que
se la llevará de paseo.
Recogerán castañas,
hojas muertas y vivas
y de pronto
la mostrará,
no para preguntarles por ella
sino para decir
que ésa era su hija
que no pudo
ser,
que no pudo recoger frutillas.

Helena Broder Commemorates the Black-and-White

She still comes close,
mutters, sighs
for that face,
for that photograph
of one who has been dead
for over three decades.
She no longer searches
among the shadows
of the hollow city,
she no longer goes to the square.

Only when she is alone,
she bends close to that photograph
to tell her that
she will take her for a stroll.
They will gather chestnuts,
dead leaves and living ones,
and suddenly
she will show it,
not to ask about her
but to say
that she was her daughter
who could not
be,
who could not pick strawberries.

Las Odiseas de Helena

Después de la osadía
del viaje,
con sus sueños del aire
más allá de las peripecias
secretas de las travesías,
como un murmullo
o el bramido suave del bosque,
he llegado a tu rostro
como quien llega al amor.

De pronto,
tus ojos,
claridades ondulantes,
ríos sin nombre
como el sueño de Dios sobre tus párpados.

Me acerco a tu frente.
Como una ciega reconozco
la tierra, sus inconclusas
geografías, sus guerras de sombras rojizas.

Soy tu casa,
el corazón
del bosque,
el mar líquido
de tus ojos,
tu lengua,
la mía.
Quiero recorrer
tu memoria,

Helena's Odysseys

After the audacity
of travel,
with her dreams of air
beyond the secret
vicissitudes of the crossings,
like a murmur
or the soft howling of the forest,
I have arrived at your face
like someone who has found love.

Suddenly,
your eyes,
undulating lights,
rivers without names,
like God's dream on your eyelids.

I approach your forehead.
Like a blind woman, I recognize
the earth, its unfinished
geography, its wars of reddish shadows.

I am your abode,
the heart of
the forest,
the liquid sea
of your eyes,
your tongue,
mine.
I want to embrace
your memory,

indagar linajes.
Déjame reír contigo.
Ser cristal
entre el muro de tus
labios.

to seek out your lineage.
Let me laugh with you.
Let me be a crystal tone
on the walls of
your lips.

Los mapas de Helena

Alucinada, junto a la asombrosa
rotación de la mano
busco a mi país.
El mapa yace recostado
sobre una mesa consumida y distante
en los dominios perdidos del exilio.

Busco a mis ríos
desfigurados y amarillos
en esta geografía frágil del exilio.
No encuentro a mis amados Andes
desparramados y azules.
Encuentro ciudades que amé.
Otras figuran en la ausencia.
Las dejé casi como en el tiempo fugitivo.
Marco parajes donde leí mi primer poema,
besé fugitiva y estremecida.

La cartografía indica precisos
parajes, valles olvidados,
montañas y grutas,
ciudades donde la historia
irrumpió su destino atroz.
Yo busco lo que el mapa esconde:
lo que no dicen las fronteras amarillas,
patios y limoneros,
caricias y lenguaje,
un silencio tibio de brisas,
la llegada a la casa de la playa
con la sal en el rostro,

Helena's Maps

Stunned, tied to the amazing
circling of my hand,
I look for my country.
The map lies
on a decrepit, distant table
in the lost dominions of exile.

I search for my rivers
disfigured and yellow
in this fragile geography of exile.
I cannot find my beloved Andes,
scattered and blue.
I find cities I have loved.
Others remain absent.
I left them behind, as if in a fugitive time.
I trace places where I read my first poem,
when I kissed furtive and trembling.

Cartography shows precise
landscapes, forgotten valleys
mountains and grottos,
cities where history
erupted with its harrowing destiny.
I search for what the map hides,
what the yellow borders do not say,
patios and lemon trees,
caresses and words of love,
a warm silence of breezes,
the arrival at the house by the sea,
the face full of salt,

con la memoria del agua que
es un cielo de palabras.

Aquí tan lejos
el mapa es un hallazgo misterioso.
Me asegura que vivo en
otro hemisferio, que
esta lengua que hoy hablo no es la mía
ni yo soy yo en ella.

Yo fui de otros ríos,
de un caminar mesurado y centelleante,
una adolescencia de brumas y fuegos salvajes.

Este mapa me asegura
la permanencia de mi propia dudosa
supervivencia,
pero no tiene mi historia.
No se acomoda a mi regazo.
Alucinada me encuentro en
una geografía que no es la mía.
Recibo postales a una dirección donde creo que vivo
y donde nadie me visita.

Sigo buscando con una fe enloquecida
lo que fue de aquella casa
con puertas llenas de dicha
y persigo mi uniforme azul de colegio
muerto en alguna silla escuálida.

the memory of water that
is a sky of words.

Here, so far away,
the map is a mysterious discovery.
It assures me that I live in
another hemisphere, that
this language I speak today is not mine
nor can I be myself in it.

I belonged to other rivers,
to a measured and shining walk,
an adolescence of mists and wild fires.

This map assures me
of the permanence of my own doubtful
survival,
but it does not have my history.
Stunned, I find myself
in a borrowed, fugitive geography
that does not belong to me.
I receive postcards at an address where I believe I live
and where nobody visits me unannounced.

I am searching with maddened faith
for what became of that house
with doors full of happiness
and I seek out my blue school uniform,
dead on some flimsy chair.

La carta de Helena Broder

I.

Encendida y deseosa
la aguardo como
quien reconoce las
danzantes acrobacias
del amor.
Inclinada, amatoria
la pienso,
la oigo,
la siento sonora y dulce
como la memoria
irreverente.

II.

Esta carta,
una cascada luminosa
de los sueños.
Sé que está viajando,
que ha cruzado innumerables
distancias,
que su destino no es el de las
fronteras
ni de los policías desalmados.
Ella es ágil, sedosa,
coqueta, centelleante.

Helena Broder's Letter

I.

Ablaze and eager
I wait for it like
someone who recognizes the
dancing acrobatics
of love.
Leaning lovingly,
I think of it,
hear it,
resounding and sweet
like irreverent
memory.

II.

This letter,
a luminous cascade
of dreams.
I am certain of its journeys,
distant crossings.
Its destiny is not that of
war-torn borders
or heartless policemen.
It is agile, silky,
coquettish, sparkling.

III.

Ella demora en sus peregrinaciones,
pero ama esa lentitud
y esa espera tan sin premura,
esa espera como los lazos del aire.
De pronto
alguien la trae hasta mi puerta
en todos los calendarios,
más allá de todas las estaciones
y me perfumo toda
antes de abrirla.
Me preparo toda
en ese instante,
violeta,
como quien aguarda al viejo amor sin escrúpulos.
Me siento en el cuarto más secreto
donde ardían tan sólo mis buenos y perversos deseos.
Allí en un manto de hojas del siempre otoño,
entre las luminosas espesuras
de la paz y el insomnio,
la abro.
Lleva la letra de amigos y conocidos.
Alguien la labró con sus manos de rey labriego,
o prisionero.
Me dicen que es de un leproso,
quizás de Isla de Pascua,
de un amante clandestino.
Lleva las más bellas imperfecciones de las letras,
como los destinos.
Me detengo en sus oleajes,
en sus grandes y pequeñas anécdotas.

III.

It takes time on its pilgrimage,
loving slowness
and the waiting without haste,
waiting like ribbons of air.
Suddenly,
somebody brings it to my open door,
in all calendars,
beyond all seasons
and I sprinkle myself with perfume
before opening it.
I prepare myself completely
in that violet
instant,
like someone waiting for love without inhibitions.
I sit in the most secret of chambers,
where only my good and perverse desires are burning.
There, over a blanket of leaves from the perpetual autumn,
amid the luminous density
of peace and insomnia,
I open it.
It has the handwriting of friends and acquaintances.
Somebody traced it with the hands of a laborer king
or prisoner.
They tell me that it is from a leper,
perhaps from Easter Island,
from a clandestine lover.
Beautiful imperfections mark the writing,
like destinies.
I halt before its waves,
its long and short anecdotes.

Entonces, después de las numerosas lecturas
después de meditar las posibles verdades,
la guardo en mi corazón,
en mi bolsillo encantado.

IV.

Es tu carta,
o tal vez la mía,
viajada, sorprendida, cercana y lejana.
Es una carta amada
que llega a las puertas de mi casa
que es el pequeño palacio de todos los secretos.
Es una carta
como el impaciente timbre de la lluvia,
como las hojas,
las plumas,
las alegrías de la fe.
Está tallada en letras de árboles y pájaros.
Es una carta de alas,
una carta de bosques y magas invisibles.
Yo la leo
en voz alta y secreta
y me alegro que haya caído en la cavidad de mis manos
una carta de amor, para estos labios oscuros;
una carta,
para aplacar el futuro incierto;
una carta sin premura
como son todas las cartas:
el privilegio del amor.

Then, after numerous readings,
after meditating on the possible truths,
I keep it in my heart,
in my enchanted pocket.

IV.

It is your letter,
or maybe mine,
traveled, surprised, near and far.
It is a beloved letter
that arrives at the door of my house,
the small palace of all secrets.
A letter resonating
like the impatient drumming of rain,
like leaves,
feathers,
the joys of faith.
A letter of birds and trees.
A wingèd letter,
a letter of forests and invisible fairies.
I read it
both aloud and secretly
and I am happy that it has fallen into the cup of my hands
a love letter, for these dark lips;
a letter,
to appease the uncertain future;
a letter written without haste
as all letters are:
the privilege of love.

Conversaciones con Dios y Helena Broder

Era muy breve el encantamiento,
asombrado el asombro
cuando me encontré con Dios
esta mañana.
Después de interminables hazañas y disputas
me reconcilié con su aliento,
con sus manos de viento
sobre mi nuca.

Le dije, soy lo
que soy.
Soy una judía
que se pelea
contigo;
una judía
que no comprende
por qué arden en mis ojos
las aldeas de Lituania,
las celdas de Terezin,
los cuerpos amontonados
de Rwanda.

Dios, sentado frente a mí
no dijo nada.
Enmudeció.
Anunció que era su presencia
sin respuesta,
aunque con interrogantes.

Conversations with God and Helena Broder

The enchantment was very brief,
I was stunned, astonished
when I met God
this morning.
After unending feats and quarrels
I reconciled myself with his breath,
with his hands of wind
on the back of my neck.

I told him, I am
what I am.
I am a Jew
wrestling
with you;
a Jew
who does not understand
why in my eyes burn
the villages of Lithuania,
the cells of Terezin,
the piled up bodies
of Rwanda.

God, seated in front of me,
said nothing.
He was silent.
He announced that his presence
had no answers,
but questions.

Sin embargo,
la prueba más fuerte
de la supervivencia,
el milagro de ser,
fue sentir su aliento sobre mis palmas
y ser yo también estela de los orígenes.

Así como el amor que crece
y no se deshoja,
empecé a creer.
Recité un salmo.
Me acomodé el cabello
y canté.
El viento de Dios
me anunció las palabras.

However,
the strongest proof
of survival,
the miracle of being,
was to feel his breath on my palms
and to be a path to the origin.

Just like love that grows
and does not fade,
I started to believe.
I chanted a psalm.
I fixed my hair,
singing.
The wind of God
announced the words to me.

La ceremonia del adiós

I.

Entra el día a tus ojos
velados por la quietud sagrada
de una muerte deseada,
tu hijo cubre los espejos,
las gruesas maderas del portón
gimen por tu ausencia.
Te llevan de la casa, Helena Broder.
Pareces una diadema
en tu cama de tules y plumas mansas.

II.

Me despido de lejos, Helena.
Me han dicho que los niños
no deben ser amigos de la muerte.
No me dejan ni besar esa frente,
esos cabellos de sedas claras
que tantas veces se enredaron en mis manos,
más grandes que las tuyas.

III.

Te vas, Helena Broder
y las palomas ya no regresarán al balcón
y tan sólo la ausencia de tus pasos
invocará tu presencia.

Pasan los años, Helena.
Nos hemos mudado de país
y de idioma.

The Ritual of Goodbye

I.

Daylight filters into your eyes,
veiled by the sacred stillness
of a welcome death
as your son covers the mirrors
and the heavy wooden gates
wail your absence.
They take you from the house, Helena Broder.
You look like a diadem
in your bed of tulles and eiderdowns.

II.

I say goodbye from afar, Helena.
They tell me that children
do not know how to greet death.
They do not even let me kiss your forehead,
those locks of clear silk
that so many times covered my hands,
bigger than yours.

III.

You are going, Helena Broder,
and the doves will not return to the balcony,
only the absence of your steps
shall invoke your presence.

Years go by, Helena.
We have changed our country
and our language.

El espejo fabricó un rostro más turbio
y el cielo que antes mirábamos
es un parche desconocido.

Te he añorado todos estos años, Omamá Helena.
Regresé a Viena
para reconocerte
y no te vi en el rostro de las otras ancianas.
Eran ellas las que te habían matado.
Las supe perdonar.
Callé mi ira
y por las noches encendí velas.
Conjuré a tus primas
y sobre todo,
bendije tu nombre
que me rozaba las manos
esas tardes de Viena
cuando compartí mi memoria con la lluvia.

The mirror reflected a clouded face
and the sky at which we once gazed
is unfamiliar.

I have missed you, Omamá Helena.
I returned to Vienna
to recognize you
in the faces of other old ladies.
They were the ones that killed you.
I learned to forgive them.
I silenced my rage,
and at night I lit candles.
I called on your dead cousins,
and especially
I blessed your name
that grazed my hands
on those evenings of Vienna.
when I shared my memory with the rain.

Ella

Ella
pregunta,
indaga sobre genealogías,
fracturados linajes.
Un árbol de la vida desnudo,
ligero de historias.

Se mira al espejo
intenta rescatar gestos,
el color de los ojos que no conoció
o la paz de los sueños
antes de la guerra,
antes cuando el tiempo era sereno y noble.

Pregunta por su historia,
por el nombre de sus abuelos.
Busca anochecida
mapas anochecidos,
tan solo encuentra raíces
grietas en las fechas,
tinieblas en el recuerdo,
cumpleaños no celebrados,
una vida suspendida en
las preguntas.

Un día
los encuentra
en el silencio de Auschwitz,
en la perversidad de Auschwitz,
en la complicidad de Auschwitz.

She

She
questions,
inquires into genealogies,
fractured lineages.
A bare tree of life
bereft of stories.

She looks at the mirror
attempting to rescue the gestures,
the color of those eyes she never knew,
or the peace of dreams
before the war,
before when time was peaceful and noble.

She questions her fate,
asks about her grandparents' names.
At dusk she searches
the darkened maps,
only to find roots
hidden among the dates,
dimly remembered
birthdays, never celebrated,
a life suspended in
questions.

One day
she finds them
in the silence of Auschwitz,
in the perversity of Auschwitz,
in the complicity of Auschwitz.

Se inclina
sobre la tierra,
se desmaraña el cabello,
se raja los vestidos rojos,
reza el Kaddish
por ellos y por ella.

Por fin los encuentra
y su imaginación ya a nada le teme
se los imagina sentados
con sus semblantes bondadosos,
se imagina sus voces y sus pasos.

Aquí en esta tierra acechada por el odio y el olvido
recobra su nombre,
el de sus abuelos
y los nombra una y otra vez,
reza el Kaddish.

A lo lejos la muerte sale a su encuentro,
dios sale a su encuentro
pero no tienen nada que decir.
Nieva en la ciudad de los muertos,
los niños juegan con la nieve y las cenizas
aunque ella no ve ningún fuego,
tan solo a los judíos muertos
envueltos en sus chales para el rezo.

Ha encontrado su genealogía
regresa a su casa,
a sus amigas,
les cuenta de sus abuelos.

She leans
on the earth,
untangles her hair,
tears her red clothes,
says Kaddish
for them as well as for her.

Finally she finds them
and her imagination no longer fears anything,
she sees them sitting down
with their kind faces,
she imagines their voices and their footsteps.

Here in this land threatened by hatred and amnesia,
she recovers her name,
her grandparents' name,
she names them over and over again,
says Kaddish.

Far away, death comes to meet her,
god comes to meet her
but they have nothing to say.
It snows in the city of the dead,
children play with snow and ashes
still, she sees no fire,
only dead Jews
wrapped in their prayer shawls.

She has found out her genealogy,
she returns home
to her friends,
she tells them about her grandparents.

Tu rostro

Un día
te encontrarás
con tu rostro,
leal historia de tu
origen y tu ruta.
Te reconocerás en él
y sentirás ternura,
la imperfección de las fisuras
del ojo que como un corazón
palpita.

Sentirás que el paso de los años
es aún leve,
no te verás como una anciana ni más
carcomida;
todo lo contrario, tu rostro,
en la plenitud del reconocimiento
te dará la diáfana luz de todos los comienzos.

Te detendrás en los cabellos que caen
armoniosos
hasta tocar tus sienes.
Son blancos y a veces dorados,
hábiles filtradores de luz y oscuridad.

Te mirarás la piel
con sus grietas traviesas con
el rictus de tu boca
que marca siempre la ilusión
de todos los cumpleaños.

Your Face

One day
you will encounter
your face,
faithful history of your
origin and your path.
You will recognize yourself in it
and will feel tenderness,
the imperfection of fissures,
the eye like a beating
heart.

You will feel the weight of years
is still light,
you will not see yourself as an old woman
consumed;
on the contrary, your face,
in the fullness of awareness
will reflect the bright light of all the beginnings.

You will pause as your
hair falls softly
to touch your temples.
The white and sometimes golden strands
filter light and darkness.

You will gaze at your skin
with its mischievous wrinkles,
the grin of your mouth,
always signaling the illusion of
each birthday.

Llegarás a tus labios que han palpado
la fragancia de un cuerpo y una frente
como un horizonte desnudo.
Reconocerás cuando probaste por primera vez el deseo
y pensaste que era como beber al mar.

Tus orejas parecidas a dos caracoles
distraídos sobre la playa,
tu nariz que reconocía el sabor
del amor desde la lejanía,
y sabrás perdonarte
porque los errores son gracia divina,
necesarios faros de los embarques
y los desembarques.

Y sabrás reconocer en tu rostro el de tu
madre y el de tu hija,
el de una mujer encinta
y una anciana
que aún no comprende
la llegada de la guerra por su pueblo
ni el anuncio de los muertos.
Pero sí sabrás cuando florecen las mimosas
y el poder seductor de las lavandas.

Tu rostro siempre ha sido el mejor amigo
desde que naciste y el gesto redentor fue
mirarlo mirar tus manos,
querer sujetarlo todo con manos diminutas
como ahora cuando juegas con tus hijos,
con tus nietos,
ahora al estar más enamorada de la ilusión
que del amor.

You will arrive at your lips that have felt
the fragrance of a body and a forehead
like a naked horizon.
You will remember when you tasted
desire for the first time
and thought it was like drinking the sea.

Your ears resembling two forgotten
shells on the beach,
your nose, able to recognize
the taste of love from afar,
and you will forgive yourself
because mistakes are divine graces,
necessary lighthouses of sailings
and landings.

And you will recognize in your face
that of your mother and daughter,
a pregnant woman
and an old woman
still trying to understand
the arrival of war to her people
or the news of the dead.
But she will know when the mimosas bloom
and the seductive power of lavender.

Your face has always been your best friend,
and the saving gesture was to contemplate it,
looking at your hands,
wanting to hold everything in your tiny hands,
as you do now when you play with your children,
your grandchildren,
now that you are even more in love with
the illusion of love.

Y de pronto
te sentirás dichosa de haber vivido medio siglo
y en este asombroso y glorioso planeta
has optado por la dicha,
has optado por el amor que no pide
recompensas.
Y esta noche has amado como nunca.
Sola, te contemplas en el espejo mágico que predica
tu historia
y te encuentras cómoda en tu piel con un deseo
que parpadea dentro
de ti.

Hoy te reconoces y celebras tu fiesta.
Todos los días decides jugar con el universo,
festejar las estrellas,
el viento que juega con tu cabello de sal y soles,
con tus manos de agua y sombras.

And suddenly
you will feel joyful for having lived
half a century on this amazing and glorious planet.
You have chosen joy,
opted for a love that does not
demand other rewards.
And tonight you have loved as never before.
Alone, you regard yourself in the magic mirror
foretelling your history
and you find yourself comfortable
in your own skin with desire
beating within you.

Today you recognize this and rejoice in your fiesta.
Each day you decide to play with the universe,
to celebrate the stars,
the wind that plays with your hair of salt and sun,
with your hands of water and shadows.

Tus manos

Turbada ante los días largos,
juegas con tus manos
pequeñas hendiduras,
opacas y tristes.

La ancianidad la marcan tus manos,
manchadas y dormidas,
grietas de la memoria,
grietas de la ternura.

Te beso las manos,
encuentro en ellas
caracoles adormecidos,
tu piel es un topacio en reposo.

Pequeña niña, vieja
como los dedales y las diademas
acaricio tus manos,
las yemas adormecidas,
encuentro en ellas
la más misteriosa de las geografías,
la lealtad de la vida.

Your Hands

Perplexed by the long days,
you play with your hands,
small hollows,
opaque and sad.

Your spotted hands,
stained and motionless,
cracked with memory,
cracked with tenderness.

I kiss your hands
to find in them
sleeping shells,
a skin peaceful like a topaz.

A small child, I kiss
your hands, old thimbles and diadems,
I caress your hands,
the sleeping fingertips,
to find in them
the most mysterious of geographies,
the loyalty of life.

La casa de la memoria

I.

En la casa de la memoria,
que almacena historias
de jardines oscuros,
desoladas historias
de un silencio que se
arrastra entre los muertos,
buscas
el nombre de tu pueblo
incendiado,
donde tu abuela
te abrazaba al regresar
de la escuela
y donde soñabas alguna vez
con ser novia.

Ahora tus manos se confunden
con tus labios
que humedecidos recorren las aldeas de
tu memoria,
quizás nuestra.

II.

Tan sólo un nombre
de un villorrio
en Galicia,
cerca de Polonia,
o Austria.

The House of Memory

I.

In the house of memory,
stories of dark gardens
are gathered,
desolate stories
of silence
crawling among the dead.
You look for
the name of your people
incinerated,
where your grandmother
hugged you when you returned
from school,
and where sometimes you dreamed
of being a bride.

Now, your hands join
your moistened lips
as they pass by the hamlets of
your memory,
maybe ours.

II.

Only the name
of a small town
in Galicia,
close to Poland,
or Austria.

La geografía también es oscura,
tan sólo la certeza de los muertos
nombra a tu pueblo,
al de tu abuela,
que soñaba con los unicornios,
que aún parece llamarte
entre las hojas de aquel jardín
entre las sombras,
y tú untas tus labios
en el muro de los recuerdos.

III.

Besas un nombre
de un pueblo en llamas,
como cuando pequeña besabas
el Sidur
en una sinagoga perdida de América del Sur,
donde pudiste soñar con ser novia,
y en una memoria de instante diáfano
tu abuela apareció entre las sombras del humo,
y te bendijo.

IV.

En las amanecidas,
la zona de la poesía desciende
sobre las horas claras.
Mi mano palpa esta divina
presencia,
gloria humilde, fecunda.

The geography is equally dark,
only the certainty of death
names your people.
Your grandmother,
who dreamt of unicorns,
still seems to call you
amid the leaves of that garden
among shadows,
and you anoint your lips
on the wall of remembrances.

III.

You kiss the name
of a people on fire,
just as when you were little
and you kissed the Sidur
in a lost synagogue of South America,
where you dreamed of being a bride,
and in the memory of a clear instant
your grandmother appeared among the
shadows of smoke,
and blessed you.

IV.

At dawn,
the space of poetry comes
in the clear hours.
My hand feels this divine
presence,
humble, fertile glory.

Deslizo mis dedos sobre las palabras
como si cada una de ellas
fuese una historia de amor,
fragancia entre las sílabas.
Tejo palabras,
olas diáfanas sobre la hoja,
quieta, recojo el dictado.
Y tú, al otro lado de la letra,
en la sonora claridad de la luz,
sonríes.

La poesía es la historia del amor,
llama presente,
para acallar la soledad de los que se aman
a oscuras.

My fingers glide over the words,
as if each one of them
were a love story,
a fragrance among syllables.
I knit words,
luminous waves over the page,
calmly, I take dictation.
And you, on the other side of the words,
in the resonant clarity of light,
smile.

Poetry is the story of love,
eternal flame
to mitigate the solitude of those who love
each other in the dark.

Les Milles

A mi padre

Nunca nos hablaste de Marsella
ni del desamparo de tu nacimiento
en una ciudad de puerto humilde,
de miradas precarias.

Nunca regresaste a Marsella
ni nos dejaste regresar a ella
custodiando tu dolor y el nuestro.

Poco supimos de esos primeros pasos,
de ese sueño extraño y extranjero,
y, sin embargo,
el ángel del azar
te llevó a Chile,
donde descalzo bajaste en un
frágil velero.

Si te hubieras quedado en Marsella
no hubieras sido mi padre.
Estarías recostado entre la distante memoria de
las cenizas.
Y antes de *Les Milles*
junto a los judíos de Marsella,
huéspedes silenciosos
a la espera de la muerte,
a la espera del pito anunciador del
tren
que no te dejará jamás regresar a Marsella
ni a ninguna ciudad de puerto triste.

Les Milles

To my father

You never spoke about Marseille
or the neglect of your birth
in a humble port city,
of precarious gazes.

You never returned to Marseille
or allowed us to return to her
guarding your pain and ours.

Little did we know of those first steps,
of that strange and foreign dream,
and yet,
the angel of chance
carried you to Chile
where you descended barefoot
from a fragile sailing ship.

If you had remained in Marseille
you would not have been my father.
You would be leaning against the distant memory
of ashes.
Before *Les Milles*,
together with the Jews of Marseille,
silent guests
waiting for death,
waiting for the whistle announcing
the train
that would never let you return to Marseille
or any other sad port city.

Este verano regreso también a Marsella
pero viajo de paso.
Soy tu hija,
e hija en el más recóndito origen.
También temo a los puertos sombríos,
a las miradas esquivas,
a un mar más cercano al lodo.
Y sin embargo
me hubiera gustado caminar por la ciudad
que te vio nacer.
Tal vez sentarme en una esquina
y sentir la espesa hendidura de las lágrimas
por ti,
por nuestra vida salvada,
por el azar que te llevó a Chile y no
a *Les Milles.*
Tal vez me hubiera gustado
ser como todos
amadora de los placeres
más ligera en el
aprendizaje de la memoria.
Pero me fue difícil no mirar
hacia atrás
ni sepultar la imagen de los otros.
Desde Marsella a Les *Milles*
dirección a Auschwitz
también ruta de navegación sombría
donde nada ni nadie alumbra ni llegadas ni
regresos.

En casa de Marsella no se habla
pero si de otro puerto amado,
Valparaíso y sus luces serpentinas.

This summer I also return to Marseille
but I am just passing through.
I am your daughter,
daughter in the most profound of origins,
I am also afraid of darkened ports,
furtive gazes,
a sea closer to mud.
And yet
I would have loved to walk through the city
that saw your birth.
Maybe, to sit by a corner
and feel the thick fissure of tears
shed for you,
for our salvaged life,
for a chance occurrence that took you to Chile and not
to *Les Milles*.
To be like everyone,
a lover of pleasures
lighter in the
apprenticeship of memory.
But it was hard for me not to look back
or bury the image of all the others.
From Marseille to *Les Milles*
heading for Auschwitz,
another somber itinerary
where nothing or no one shed light on the arrivals or
returns.

At home we do not talk of Marseille
but of Valparaíso, another beloved port,
and its strings of lights.

Pesaj en Chile

Esta noche,
distinta a las
demás noches,
regresa la primavera
a sus dominios de jazmines.
Esta noche,
distinta a las
demás noches,
nos inclinamos sobre los lugares
donde la memoria
de otro tiempo
también se reclinaba.
Nuestro aprendizaje yace en el canto.

Los más jóvenes preguntan:
¿por qué ésta noche
no es como las demás noches?
Los mayores repiten:
porque también nosotros fuimos esclavos
en las tierras de Egipto
y el jazmín unta los labios
y el canto es fragancia.
Nuestro aprendizaje yace en el canto.

Mi hijo lee de la Hagadah.
El tuyo responde.
Trenzas de voces,
jardines inquietos
como palabras
y es esta historia un gesto en el regazo
del origen.
Nuestro aprendizaje yace en el canto.

Passover in Chile

Tonight,
unlike all
other nights,
spring returns
to its dominions of jasmine.
Tonight,
unlike all
other nights,
we contemplate the places
where the memory
of another time
also sleeps.
What we have learned springs forth in song.

The youngest ones ask:
Why is tonight
different from all other nights?
The elders repeat:
Because we were also slaves
in the land of Egypt
and jasmine moistens our lips
making our chants fragrant.
What we have learned springs forth in song.

My son reads from the Haggadah.
Yours responds.
Braided voices,
restless gardens
like words
and this history is a gesture in the lap
of our beginnings.
What we have learned springs forth in song.

Tu hija abre la puerta
para que lleguen los extranjeros,
las mujeres con canastas vacías.
Mi hija abre la ventana para soñar
con los tiempos de la miel y del trigo,
o un cielo abierto como el Alef,
cielo de las fronteras imaginarias.

El cielo es distinto esta noche,
no es como las otras noches,
alado, cubierto del rezo,
suave como un canto sobre la
sombra de Dios.
Nombramos las estrellas
y repetimos el nombre de aquellos campos
donde nosotros también morimos:
Bergen Belsen, Dachau, Treblinka,
Auschwitz.

Esta noche es como todas las otras noches
soñamos con el amor
o el tiempo donde las mujeres recogían olivos
y cantaban sobre la paz.

El anciano de la mesa redonda,
un rey Arturo judío
murmura, gime o reza.
Bendice el vino y sus lumbres,
la tierra y sus antorchas de fiesta.
Cantamos
inclinados
sobre la Hagadah de Sarajevo
o de Alejandría

Your daughter opens the door
for the arrival of the foreigners,
the women with empty baskets.
My daughter opens the window to dream
of the times of honey and wheat,
or of an open sky like the Aleph,
a heaven of imaginary borders.

The sky is different tonight,
unlike other nights,
it is winged, shielded by prayers,
soft as a song about
the shadow of God.
We name the stars
and repeat the name of those camps
where we also died:
Bergen Belsen, Dachau, Treblinka,
Auschwitz.

Tonight, like all other nights
we dream of love,
or of the time when women gathered olives
and sang about peace.

The old man of the round table,
a Jewish King Arthur,
whispers, moans or prays.
He blesses the wine and its lights,
the land and its festive torches.
We sing,
leaning
over the Haggadah of Sarajevo
or Alexandria

y el viento de Dios recorre
nuestras mejillas
untadas por la sal,
agradecidas y plenas.

Esta noche tan distinta a las demás noches;
esta noche donde yo te amo, extranjero,
mi cuerpo te recibe
como si tú fueras también un pueblo perdido.

and the wind of God passes across
our cheeks
anointed by salt,
grateful and satisfied.

This night so different from all other nights;
this night where I love you, a foreigner,
my body welcomes you
as if you were also a lost people.

Torá

Como agua viva
y huerto sembrado,
enhebro mi mano
sobre tu rostro
en el acto de la fe.

Danzas ligeramente sobre el cuerpo de los
que amas.
Eres una reina cautelosa.
Haces pequeñas reverencias.
Eres cascabel que anuncia lo sagrado del día
y cargadora fugaz de rituales.

Segura en tu peregrino quehacer,
toda vestida de colores
te despliegas.
Eres un soplo sobre
los párpados de dios,
un viento sobre los olivares.

Te beso en tu cima clara.
Toda turbia me ruborizo ante
la mutua presencia.
Eres novia del sábado
y de las fiestas sagradas;
el libro de Dios;
el libro de los hombres:
Torah.
Dorada y vacilante
en tu alfabeto
soy un alma en mil espejos.

Torah

Like living water
and fertile orchard,
I thread my hand
over your face
in the gestures of faith.

You dance gently over your loved ones.
You are a benign queen,
making little curtsies.
You are a bell announcing the sacredness of day,
fleeting carrier of rituals.

Confident in your itinerant life,
all dressed in colors,
you unfurl.
You are a gust of wind
in God's eye,
a breeze
through the olive trees.

I kiss your clear crown.
All misty I flush before
our mutual presence.
You are the bride of Saturday
and of holy days;
God's book,
man's book:
Torah.
Golden and hesitant
in your alphabet,
I am a soul in a thousand mirrors.

Sukkot

La luz irradia
sobre el jardín hechizado.
Tu mirada también ya otra
se asemeja a lo que se re-encuentra,
senderos entrecortados.

Esta es noche de aromas,
aromas que nacieron antes de tu niñez.
Tu madre te enseñó a repetir la palabra "Etrog"
"Lulav".
El hebreo de Dios se ondula en tus labios,
son los labios de Dios.
Juegas y amas la fe.
La estación de las hojas revoloteando en tus pies.

Estás hecha de memorias,
intervalos de un sueño,
estrellas y tiempos fugaces,
huidas para poder soñar con el regreso.

La Suka es precaria y frágil,
hecha de hojas muertas
y vivas.
Siempre los resquicios de luz desfilan
por el cielo que desde niña amaste
cuando empezaste a nombrar estrellas.

La noche es como una noche de agua viva.
La noche de Sukkot después de la desgarradora noche
de Yom Kippur.

Sukkot

Light radiates
over the bewitching garden.
Your gaze, already different,
resembles what we encounter again,
paths intertwined.

This is a night full of aromas,
scents born before your childhood.
Your mother taught you to repeat words like "Etrog,"
"Lulav."
God's Hebrew curves your lips,
they are God's lips.
You play and love your faith,
the season of leaves fluttering around your feet.

You are made of memories,
intervals of a dream,
stars and fleeting times,
flights that enable the dream of a return.

The Sukkah is precarious and fragile,
made of leaves,
dead and living.
Fragments of light always shine
through the childhood sky that you so loved
when you began to name the stars.

Tonight is like a night of living water.
The night of Sukkot, after the heartrending night
of Yom Kippur.

Ahora se aliviana el alma,
danzas alrededor de las palmas.
El Etrog lo estrechas junto a tu corazón
como a las cosas que más amas.
Y en la precariedad de la Suka
entiendes la transitorio
y frágil de las paredes,
la vulnerabilidad de los objetos.

Descubres después de tantas migraciones
que tú eres una.
Se acomoda a la geografía de tu rostro.
La acomodas en tus manos como antes
a tus hijos pequeños
y ahora a tus poemas que esparces como si fueran especies.

Brilla esta noche la Suka
como brillan las cosas afianzadas por el amor.
Brindas por los muertos y los vivos,
pronuncias sus nombres
y te dejas llevar por las presencias,
por lo que el alfabeto no dice.
Comprendes que los ángeles de la memoria
visitan a la Suka esta noche
y crees en las alas de las mariposas
porque sí son el alma de los muertos.

Amas las cosas precarias,
lo inefable,
el amor que te llega de pronto
como un susurro sobre el aliento de Dios.
Esta noche, esta primera noche de Sukkot
con un cielo que derrama estrellas,
es una noche sin olvidos.

Now the soul comes alive,
you dance among the palms,
holding the Etrog close to your heart
like the things you love the most.
And in the shaky frame of the Sukkah
you understand impermanence,
the fragility of walls,
the vulnerability of objects.

After so many migrations, you realize
that you are home.
It fits the geography of your face.
You fit it in your hands as you did before
holding your small children,
and now your poems, that you spread like spices.

Tonight the Sukkah shines
like objects on which love has a firm hold.
You toast both the dead and the living,
you pronounce their names
and let yourself be carried by their presence,
by what the alphabet does not mention.
You understand that the angels of memory
visit the Sukkah tonight
and you believe in the wings of butterflies
because they are the souls of the dead.

You love precarious things,
what cannot be spoken,
love when it arrives suddenly
like a whisper of God's breath.
Tonight is the first night of Sukkot
with sky spreading stars,
a night free of cares.

La noche de Auschwitz

I.

En la inocencia de un paisaje incierto,
en la oscuridad de la noche de Auschwitz
la imaginación se desborda
o ya no imagina,
se cierra como una coraza.
En la oscuridad de la noche de Auschwitz
los caminos trastornados se
transforman en sombras
y anuncian la llegada de los
muertos.

II.

En la oscura noche de Auschwitz
los muertos ni lloran ni sonríen,
regresan sin mensajes, sin memoria.
Se acuerdan de los carromatos de la muerte,
tan sólo ellos se cierran sus ojos,
desbordados y abiertos.

En este día de los muertos
donde los cristianos visitan los cementerios
con exquisitas ofrendas,
pienso en la solitaria noche de Auschwitz,
en un cielo de peces muertos
y aves francotiradoras.

El espectáculo es un escenario inimaginable,
igual lo imagino:

Night at Auschwitz

I.

In the innocence of an uncertain landscape,
in the darkness of the night at Auschwitz,
imagination overflows
or is unable to imagine
and it closes up like a shell.
In the dark night of Auschwitz,
tortured paths
are transformed into shadows
announcing the arrival of
the dead.

II.

In the dark night of Auschwitz,
the dead neither cry nor smile,
they return without messages or memory.
They remember the wagons of the dead
and only they close their eyes,
overflowing and open.

On this Day of the Dead
when Christians visit cemeteries
with exquisite offerings,
I think of the lonely night at Auschwitz,
a sky with dead fish
and sniping birds.

The show is an unimaginable stage,
yet I still imagine it:

es un teatro con la delicada urgencia del mal.
Llegan a esta noche del mal
los muertos
a sabiendas que ya poco se les recuerda
y regresan no a marcar tumbas
ni a desafiar memorias
tan sólo vuelven
al lugar que más conocen,
la zona de la muerte,
los carromatos donde instalaban sus cuerpos,
brazos, piernas, uñas,
cabellos deshojados.

A veces recogen a los otros muertos,
los que quedaron más atrás,
los que nadie subió al vagón de la muerte.
Tan solo, y tal vez por eso,
en las noches de Auschwitz,
los muertos regresan.
Los hemos visto,
tienen miedo,
tienen frío.
Siempre es invierno en Auschwitz.
Pero a veces desnudos caminan
rumbo al sol,
o a abrir los ojos de los vivos.

Sueño con esta noche de Auschwitz
y con mi abuela y sus camisas de alquimias.

a theater with the delicate urgency of evil.
The dead come to this night
of evil
knowing that they are hardly remembered,
and they return not to deface graves
or challenge memories;
they only return
to the place they know most,
the zone of death,
the wagons where their bodies were placed,
arms, legs, nails,
disheveled hair.

Sometimes they gather the other dead,
those who remained behind,
those who nobody carried to the wagon of death.
Only, and maybe because of this,
in the nights of Auschwitz,
the dead return.
We have seen them,
they are afraid,
they are cold.
It is always winter in Auschwitz.
but sometimes they walk naked
towards the sun,
or to open the eyes of the living.

I dream of this night at Auschwitz
and of my grandmother and her magical shirts.

Imaginar un navío

Imaginar un navío,
rigurosamente oscuro,
silencioso, dolido
como los pasos clandestinos
de los prófugos desdichados.

Imaginar el navío,
secreto, vigilante,
se aleja del puerto
atrás el destino de los muertos,
una Europa descompuesta.

Imaginar ese navío
y tan solo ese navío
como una melodía que se fuga
de la muerte oficial,
del castigo por el origen,
condenado por el nacimiento.

En ese navío,
que cruzará el mar de nadie,
los paisajes de la aterradora memoria,
van los judíos
descalzos, desnudos
la única pertenencia es
la posibilidad de la vida
de ser la vida
de vivir la vida.

Imagine a Ship

Imagine a ship,
absolutely dark,
silent, suffering,
like the furtive steps
of poor fugitives.

Imagine the ship,
secret, vigilant,
retreating from the port,
leaving behind the fate of the dead,
a Europe destroyed.

Imagine that ship,
and only that ship,
like a melody escaping from
a decreed death,
a punishment for your ancestry,
a death sentence for being born.

In this ship,
that will cross the nameless sea,
the scenes of horrific memory,
are the Jews
barefoot, naked,
their only possession
the possibility of life:
of being alive
of staying alive.

Van ellos audaces,
cargan candelabros de siete velas
y la memoria de la dicha.

Imaginar el navío
que oculta a las mujeres pálidas y sonámbulas
vestidas con los trajes de la muerte,
soñando con el ámbar.

Larga es esta navegación
como un abismo sin nombre
como un puente que no cruza
orillas.
Ellos, los pasajeros, imaginan las idas
atrás queda Europa bárbara y húmeda
tras las lluvias y las cenizas.

Imaginar el navío
y un chal de estrellas
un cielo de ecos y nombres
por nombrarse.

De pronto alguien dice:
Tierra
y es la tierra,
leve caricia en el viento,
juego de azar,
lengua de un dios
a hora presente.

Santo Domingo, Hispaniola
Colón y Juan de Torres.

Los judíos de antaño,
los judíos de Sefarad,
los judíos soñando con el mar

They travel bravely,
carrying seven-branched candelabras
and joyful memories.

Imagine the ship,
where pale sleepwalking women,
clothed in the garments of death,
dream of amber.

The voyage seems eternal
as if crossing some nameless abyss,
like a bridge unable to reach
any shore.
These passengers imagine setting out
leaving a brutal Europe behind, humid
with rains and ashes.

Imagine the ship
and a shroud of stars,
a sky full of echoes and names
yet to be named.

Suddenly someone calls out:
Land
and it *is* land,
a soft caress of the wind,
a game of chance,
the tongue of a god
suddenly present.

Santo Domingo, Hispaniola,
Columbus and Juan de Torres.

Redeemed
by the Jews of old,
the Jews of Sefarad,

en sus atuendos de navegantes,
rescatan.

Como una palma abierta
la tierra se abre
recibe
parpadea
ellos y ellas
todos
hunden sigilosamente los pies en la arena
y el placer es diurno y nocturno
y el placer es un diáfano deseo
alguien sueña ahora
con la vida
mira al cielo
canta.

Imaginar el navío
en este sábado de arribos dichosos
el viento murmura las sílabas de los
antepasados
las abuelas regresan con Jala tras las alambradas

Imaginar este navío
1940
los judíos han llegado a tierra
se reconocen
y abrazan
sus orígenes
el derecho a la vida
entre las claras aguas
sus corazones
cámaras que sobrevivieron y esperaron

Imaginar un navío
como una casa que flota en la luz.

the Jews dreaming the sea,
rescued in their sailor's outfits.

Like an open palm,
the land opens up,
welcoming,
scintillating.
Each and everyone of them
silently sink their feet in the sand,
and the pleasure is morning and night,
and the pleasure is a pure wish.
Somebody dreams now
of life,
looks skyward,
sings.

Imagine the ship
on this Sabbath of glorious arrivals.
The wind whispers the syllables
of our ancestors,
grandmothers
return with challa from behind barbed wire.

Imagine that ship
in 1940
as the Jews step ashore:
they recognize each other,
and embrace their origins,
their right to live
among clear waters.
Their hearts are
chambers where they survived
and hoped.

Imagine a ship,
like a house floating in the light.

Traducir es otra forma de amar

Paso a paso
el aprendizaje se
desliza,
se abre
cual amapola nocturna.

Traduzco tus palabras,
fragmentos de piel,
de historias.
Soy cuidadosa con ellas,
emergen en la oscuridad.
Yo las traduzco para hacerlas
luz,
pequeñas luciérnagas en el promontorio
de mis manos,
humildad del decir enlazado.

No sé bordar, tan sólo recoger hojas.
Todos los otoños repito la ceremonia de
recogerme a mí para después recoger
las hojas.
Ahora son palabras
que llenan otra voz
de dicha y pensamientos alados.

De verter una palabra sobre la otra,
descubrir lo que ocultas,
lo que develas,
lo que apenas se deja decir,
esplendor del decir en otra lengua.

Translating Is Another Way of Loving

Step by step,
our apprenticeship
moves slowly,
opening like a
nocturnal poppy.

I translate your words
fragments of skin,
of histories.
I am careful with them,
they emerge from dark regions.
I translate them to
bring them into the light,
small fireflies in the promontory
of my hands,
humility of entwined words.

I do not know how to embroider, only to gather leaves.
Every autumn I repeat the ceremony
of gathering myself, then gathering
the leaves.
Now they are words
filling another voice
with joy and winged thoughts.

Exquisite astonishment is this:
to render one word for another,
discovering what you conceal,
what you reveal,
that which is hardly said.

Pausada voy por tus silencios,
como si fueras un cuerpo subterráneo,
tanto has vivido bajo tierra
que hoy salgo al encuentro tuyo
en otro idioma,
un otro yo que renace en la melodía de mi patria.

¿Cómo serás en mi lengua?
Lengua que mi madre me cantaba,
lengua frente a un espejo constelado y ambiguo,
hasta adentrarme en la plenitud del sueño del olvido.

Traduzco sin olvidos
tan solo presencias de una voz sobre la otra
como una mano que se asemeja
a un jardín entre las sombras
para nacer traducida a otra luz.

Una mano semejante al musgo,
mano que se estira clarividente
en la plenitud de otra lengua, de otra voz,
cómplice de la primera voz.
Aprendo, me dejo llevar por una melodía
secreta que la hago mía,
humilde sitial de mi sentir,
ahora tuyo en mi voz.

Traducir es otra forma de amar,
dejarse llevar por las fisuras de las palabras,
sujetarlas entre las manos como quién
sujeta la vida de un recién nacido,
la belleza de saber que cada palabra
es inalcanzable
pero tal vez posible

Deliberately I move through your silences
as if you were a body underground,
so long have you resided under the earth,
greeting you today
in a different language,
a different *I* reborn in the melody of my country.

How would you be in my language?
The language my mother sang to me,
language in front of a starry and ambiguous mirror,
until I enter complete oblivion.

I translate without oblivion,
only presences of one voice over another,
like a hand that resembles
a garden in shadows,
reborn in a different light.

The hand resembles moss,
a hand that clairvoyantly stretches out
in the plenitude of another tongue,
from a different voice, accomplice to the first voice.
I learn, I allow myself to be taken by a secret
melody that becomes mine,
humble place of my emotions,
now yours in my voice.

Translating is another way of loving.
a way to be carried into the fissures of words,
holding them in your hands like someone
who holds the life of a newborn,
the beauty of knowing that each word
is unattainable
but perhaps possible

en el enjambre de voces
humanas,
en las constelaciones sin fronteras.

No sé bordar telas,
tan sólo recoger hojas como el vaivén
del nacimiento y de la muerte.
Amo a las hojas antes de morir
como las rosas antes de morir
aún son bellas en el cielo
salvaje del adiós.
Me gusta hacer collares con ellas
como tus versos.
Hacer de ellas collares
invisibles
con mis manos, urdirlas
en el simple gesto del aprendizaje del amor,
de una lengua que ama a la otra,
de una mano que ama el cuarzo de las letras,
la república solidaria de la escritura.

Reflejo de una palabra,
fuego tenue sobre una hoja vacía y plena.
Traducir es otra forma de amar.

in this cluster of human
voices,
in constellations without borders.

I do not know how to embroider cloth,
only to gather leaves like the gentle rocking
from birth to death.
I love leaves before they die,
just as roses before perishing
retain their beauty
in the savage firmament of goodbyes.
It pleases me to make necklaces of them
as I do with your verses.
To braid invisible necklaces
weaving them with my hands
in the simple gesture of learning to love
from one language that loves another.
From one hand in love with the quartz of letters,
the supportive republic of writing.

A reflection from another word,
pale fire upon a leaf, both empty and full.
Translating is another way of loving.

El árbol de la memoria

I.

Inútil indagar
por aquel árbol desmemoriado
de mi memoria.
Mi genealogía era una niña vieja,
dormida entre las ramas de un árbol perversamente
herido.
Mis primas habían quedado cautivas en los trenes,
otra prefirió el diseño de su propia muerte
mientras cosía la mortaja
y el traje de novia.

II.

Después supe que algunos
sobrevivieron,
no querían hablar,
la vida en sí era una perpetua
fatiga,
un río seco y torrentoso.

III.

Truncada,
no tuve ni árbol ni sombra,
tan solo una espeluznante memoria.

The Tree of Memory

I.

It is useless to inquire
about that forgetful tree
of my memory.
My genealogy was a childlike old woman,
asleep among the branches of a perversely
wounded tree.
My cousins had remained captive in the trains,
another chose to design her own death,
as she sewed the shroud
and the bride's gown.

II.

Later, I discovered that some of them
survived,
they did not want to talk,
life itself was a perpetual
fatigue,
a dry and turbulent river.

III.

Truncated,
I had neither tree nor shade,
only a terrifying memory.

IV.

Cuando tuve a primos y amigos
los militares los hicieron desaparecer,
sus vidas suspendidas,
sus trajes de fiestas
agazapados,
la vida un orificio con fondo turbado.

Aprendí a ser en una soledad más allá de toda
posible soledad,
me enamoré un poco de su muerte,
tal vez ella tendría cobijo para mí.
Mi madre aunque presente
sonreía lejana.
Su dolor era un murmullo
que no mermaba,
que no se secaba,
como las heridas sórdidas de los sobrevivientes.

V.

Mi hija después
me preguntó por su árbol
y las dos en el mes del invierno quieto
construimos un árbol
en una pared quieta como este paisaje
que amamos aquí en Nueva Inglaterra,
paisaje humano y posible.

Pusimos a las primas muertas,
a las que todas las noches vestidas de muerte y vida
nos visitaban,
a las que se salían de la Tora
y de los Sidurim.

IV.

When I had cousins and friends
the military made them disappear,
their lives suspended,
their party clothes
hidden,
all a depth of confusion.

I learned to live inside a solitude
beyond all known solitude,
somewhat enamored with their deaths
that offered me possible shelter.
My mother, though present,
smiled as if far away.
Her pain was a whisper
that would not diminish
or dry up,
like the festering wounds of survivors.

V.

Later, my daughter
asked me about her tree,
and in that quiet winter month the two of us
outlined a tree
on a wall, silent like this landscape
that we love here in New England,
a human and possible landscape.

We placed our dead cousins,
those who visited us at night
dressed as death and life,
the ones that came out of the Torah
and the Sidurim.

Las fuimos encontrando,
la pared floreció, se llenó de umbrales,
de portales secretos
alguien nos esperaba tras la pared,
alguien ofrecía una fiesta para nosotros.

VI.

Nadie clausuró esta vez la puerta.
Nadie dijo no visitar
y los vimos a todos:
a las primas en los trenes,
a la prima con un dedal y una píldora en la boca.
Habían regresado,
y como un poema
estaban dispuestas para nuestra llegada.

Poblada de hojas y de estrellas
nuestra familia es nuestra memoria,
un universo minúsculo que regresa hacia la vida.

We began to meet them,
the wall blossomed, filled with thresholds,
secret portals,
while behind the wall someone waited,
someone gave a party in our honor.

VI.

This time nobody locked the door.
Nobody told us not to visit them
and we saw them all:
the cousins on the trains,
the cousin with a thimble and a pill in her mouth.
They had returned,
and just like a poem
they were prepared for our arrival.

Populated by leaves and stars
our family is our memory,
a minuscule universe returning to life.

Sebastopol

Los abuelos nunca
nos contaron
de la nieve
sobre Sebastopol,
del paso de la luz
desdoblándose
ante las praderas
espesas,
como un espejo ocupando
la vastedad del silencio.

Todo lo que sé de los abuelos
es como la nieve en Sebastopol,
objetos e historias
colmados de silencio
presencias mudas en la pradera
blanca.

La nieve se regocijaba
ante el silencio de los judíos de
Sebastopol
que escondidos entre los leños
y los escombros adormecidos
miraban a esa ciudad
y a ese paisaje
que nada tenía que ver con ellos
porque los judíos de Sebastopol
apenas salían a las calles.
Eso me contó mi abuela Sonia
con una voz que buscaba reposo
con una voz como de invierno,
aguda y sola.

Sebastopol

Our grandparents
never told us
about the snow
in Sebastopol,
the movement of light
filtering through thick meadows,
like a mirror
enveloping the
vastness of silence.

Everything I know about our grandparents
is like the snow in Sebastopol,
objects and stories
filled with silence,
mute presences in
white meadows.

Snow rejoiced
before the silence of the Jews of
Sebastopol
who were in hiding among the logs
and asleep in the rubble,
who looked at that city
and landscape
that had nothing to do with them
because the Jews of Sebastopol
hardly went out into the streets.
My grandmother Sonia told me this
with a voice yearning to rest,
a wintry voice,
high-pitched and alone.

Tal vez fue su voz
mi único recuerdo del invierno sobre Sebastopol,
de la nieve a la deriva,
de los pasos de los abuelos
que no dejaban huellas
tan solo el silencio que los apartaba
como el caminar de la muerte
que siempre iba con ellos
en las praderas vacías de
Sebastopol.

Perhaps it was a voice
my only memory of Sebastopol in the winter,
of snow drifting,
the steps of our grandparents leaving no trace,
only silence pushing them away
like the presence of death
always among them
in the empty meadows of
Sebastopol.

Las cosas olvidadas

Te acostumbras a dejar cosas olvidadas,
huellas,
indicios,
presagios
para algún posible regreso,
piedrecillas en los umbrales.
Así te enseñó tu abuelo,
siempre piedrecillas
recostadas sobre la tierra soleada.
Necesitas recordar a tus muertos
viven junto a ti y tú junto a ellos.
Los arrastras sobre la tierra ocre,
quieren caminar contigo.
No los puedes olvidar
viajan contigo al exilio,
a las ciudades donde nadie te espera.
Con ellos aprendes a conocer las voces
sin habla,
los pasos de los que te vigilan
para que no los olvides.
Te has convertido en sus silencios,
en lo que dejaron en la tierra inconclusa.

Te encuentras en Praga,
Cracovia,
la aldea de Broder,
nadie te recibe.
De las casas incendiadas
quedan ahora jardines secretos.

Forgotten Things

You get used to leaving things behind,
traces,
signs,
omens
for a possible return,
small stones in the doorways.
Just as your grandfather taught you,
always to leave small stones,
lying on the sunny earth.
You need to remember your dead,
they live next to you, and you with them.
You drag them over the ochre earth,
they want to walk with you,
you cannot forget them,
they travel into exile with you,
to the empty cities where nobody waits for you.
From them you learn to recognize voices
without words,
the steps of those watching you
so as not to forget them.
You have become their silences,
what they left behind in the unfinished earth.

You are in Prague,
Krakow,
the villages of Broder;
nobody greets you.
Only secret gardens remain
of those burnt out houses.

Tan solo los muertos te responden,
te dicen que estuvieron allí,
que dejaron las cosas olvidadas para tu regreso.
ahora tú regresas para ellos.

Y llueve mucho en esta travesía
como si el diluvio de agua quisiera irrumpir sobre tu rostro.
Has regresado no sabes por qué,
ni qué buscas,
ni de qué memorias hablas.

Eres una mariposa entre los insomnios,
caminas por donde caminó tu abuela.
Llevas su pulsera de granate
y su piel de ámbar,
la encuentras en el parque rodeada de lilas.
Está viva,
te espera.
En la invisibilidad de la tarde la encuentras,
estás amilagrada.
Regresas para encontrarla
y te parece espléndida la vida
porque te has podido reconciliar en su muerte.

Te gusta dejar cosas, perderlas,
tienes la certeza de los encuentros.

Only the dead respond
telling you they were there
leaving things behind for your return.
now you return for them.

It rains heavily on this crossing
as if this deluge wanted to burst in your face.
You have returned not knowing why,
or what you are searching for,
or what your memories invoke.

You are a butterfly among insomniacs
walking wherever your grandmother walked
with her garnet bracelet
and her amber skin.
You find her in the park, surrounded by lilacs.
In the invisibility of the afternoon you meet her,
she is alive
waiting for you.
You are touched by a miracle.
You return to find her,
and life seems magnificent to you
because you are able to reconcile with death.

You love to leave things behind, to lose them,
you are certain of encounters.

La tierra

Como un llamado de bosques
o presagios entre las brumas,
regresas a la tierra
con tus trajes ocres
y tus pasos que borran huellas.
Eres tú abuela mía,
ángel de la memoria
y de la historia.
Regresas en este año nuevo
para asegurarme de la perdurabilidad
de la ternura.
Tus ojos se han vuelto espesos como la resina
de los árboles,
como la miel que cada año degustamos en la
promesa de los tiempos dulces.

Me gusta sentirme confundida ante tu presencia en la
ambigüedad de lo que es real.
Pero es real esta memoria mía de tu risa,
de tus brazos como un inmenso
candelabro de nueve velas,
el candelabro de la alegría.

Cuánto extrañar tu presencia sobre la tierra,
cuánto extrañar el beso sobre tus ojos que aleteaban,
a mi mano sobre tu corazón que era un trazo de sol,
una ráfaga de viento inquieto.

Y en este nuevo año donde los culpables
siempre piden perdón

The Earth

Like a call from the forest
or omens among the mist,
you return to the earth
with your ochre dresses
and your steps erasing footprints.
You are my grandmother,
angel of memory
and history.
This new year you return
to assure me of the endurance
of tenderness.
Your eyes have become as thick as tree sap
or the honey that each year
we taste with the promise
of sweet times.

I love to feel perplexed before you
in the ambiguity of what is real.
But my memory of your smile is real,
of your arms like an immense
candelabra of nine candles,
the candelabra of joy.

How I miss your presence on this earth,
how I miss kissing your twinkling eyes,
my hand on your heart like a ray of sun,
a gust of restless wind.

And in this new year when the
guilty ask always for forgiveness,

y las víctimas los perdonan,
yo sólo quiero sentir tu mejilla sobre la mía,
verte recostada entre los espejos
como una odalisca cometiendo imprudencias,
hablando de lo que no se debe decir, pero lo dices,
quejándote de la poca cortesía de los caballeros de ahora.

Entonces, sólo entonces, untas la miel en la jalah,
las nueces, las almendras, el cardamomo,
la buena fortuna de todos los comienzos
que son el origen de la pasión.
Porque a mi lado estás
abuela maga,
cristalina,
habitando la esperanza
en la tierra ocre
que es una menora de nueve brazos.

and the victims forgive them,
all I want is to feel your cheek touching mine.
To see you lying among the mirrors,
an indiscreet odalisque talking about what
must not be said and yet you say it,
complaining about the lack of courtesy among today's men.

Then, only then, do you spread honey on challah,
nuts, almonds and cardamom,
good fortune of all beginnings,
source of all passion.
Because you are next to me,
magician grandmother,
crystal clear,
inhabiting hope
on this ochre earth,
that is a nine-branched menorah.

Paz

La nostalgia se hizo color,
al principio un azul huidizo
ilusamente templado,
el azul del Pacífico,
efímero, vertiginoso.
Me despedí de Chile como quién
deja para siempre el sabor del mar.

Después extrañé los verdes
de Nueva Inglaterra,
verdes trenzados entre humos tibios,
verdes al renacer la primavera,
precoz
fútil, tímida.

Extrañeza de verdes espesos
color deseo, color espesura,
imaginario de tu
mirada
verde como la fe.

Ahora extraño su luz
la luz de Israel,
la luz que vi en los niños de Israel,
la luz que vi en los ancianos de Israel,
o en los jóvenes abrazados mirando apacibles.
La luz en una tarde de sábado
sobre el Mediterráneo
que nadie visitaba
que nadie habitaba,
la luz cadenciosa,
invisible de Jaffa.

Peace

Nostalgia became a color,
at first a timid blue,
naively mild,
the blue of the Pacific,
fleeting, ever-changing.
I said goodbye to Chile like someone
leaving forever the taste of the sea.

Later, I longed for the greens
of New England,
plaited greens among mild fogs,
greens of the new spring,
precocious,
futile, shy.

The surprise of those deep greens,
the color of desire, the color of thickets,
imagined in your
gaze,
green like faith.

Now I miss the light,
the light of Israel,
the light I saw in the children of Israel
or encountered in the old people of Israel,
or in the youth embracing one another with gentle looks.
The light of a Saturday afternoon
on the Mediterranean
that nobody visited,
nobody inhabited,
the lilting, invisible
light of Jaffa.

Ahora, la luz de Jerusalén
no sé si es de ámbar o de rosa,
si es violeta
o tiene sombras doradas.
Pero es la luz,
esa luz que tiernamente regresa a mi rostro,
que me ayuda a imaginar tu rostro.
Esa luz que tiene el don de la historia,
el don de la alegría,
extraña luz
la que sabe acomodarse
en la absoluta imprecisión de la memoria.
Extrañeza de luz,
la luz de Israel
como una fábula
que entreabre el rostro.

Now, I don't know
if Jerusalem's light is amber or rose,
if it is violet
or it has golden tones.
But it is the light,
the light that tenderly returns to my face,
and helps me imagine your face.
A light endowed with the gift of history,
the gift of joy,
surprising light,
able to accommodate itself
in the utter imprecision of memory.
Extraordinary light,
the light of Israel,
that opens the face
like a fable.

Jerusalén

En aquella ciudad
codiciada por la historia,
agasajada por reyes
y poetas,
en aquella ciudad
acribillada y negada
tan sólo sentí el atuendo
de la paz,
vestido ligero sobre las colinas,
ropaje de niña entre los muros.

Y entre la historia de los manuscritos
sombríos y la
historia de los amores opalinos
hice de tu rostro
una huella
imprecisa,
un sol como colina
arqueándose en tu nuca.
Y el sol acarició tu rostro,
te dejaste bañar por su humilde
luz.

Y en Jerusalén
regresaste a una casa
de la memoria
de Dios,
la memoria de un
muro,
la memoria de un suspiro,

Jerusalem

In that city
coveted by history,
lavished by kings
and poets,
in that city
riddled with bullets and denial,
all I felt was the cloak
of peace,
light garments on the hills,
girls' dresses among the walls.

And amid the history
of dark manuscripts
and the history of opaline loves,
I traced your face
like a vague
marking,
a sun like a hill
arching on your neck.
And the sun caressed your face,
you allowed yourself to be bathed by this humble
light.

And in Jerusalem
you returned to a house
of memory,
of God.
The memory
of a wall,
the memory of a sigh,

la memoria de un rezo
sobre tus ojos sellados.
La memoria de mi cuerpo
sobre el tuyo,
ángeles caídos
dejándose ser noche y luz
sobre el lecho del amor.

the memory of a prayer
on your sealed eyes.
The memory of my body
on yours,
fallen angels
letting themselves be night and day
on the bed of love.

About the Author

Marjorie Agosín is a poet, fiction writer, memoirist, anthologist, professor and human rights activist. Friends and admirers describe her as "brilliantly indefatigable." A descendant of European Jews who escaped the Holocaust and settled in Chile in 1939, she was born in Bethesda, Maryland, and raised in Santiago, Chile. The family settled in Athens, Georgia, after fleeing the madness which pervaded Chile under Pinochet's violent rise to power. Agosín earned her Ph.D. from Indiana University. A dedicated human rights activist, Agosín is a recipient of the Jeanetta Rankin Award in Human Rights, the Good Neighbor Award from the Conference of Christians and Jews, the Girl Scouts Leading Women of 2000 Award, and the United Nations Human Rights Award. Almost all of her works reflect her concern for international human rights.

In 2004, Agosín was featured by Hispanic Magazine as on of he most outstanding Latinas of the year. In 2005, she received the prestigious Women's Leadership Award from the National Hispanic Leadership Institute.

Agosín's numerous literary awards include the Letras de Oro Prize and the Latina Literature Prize. Recently she received a writing grant from the Andrew Mellon Foundation. Agosín's poetry includes *Conchalí* (1981), *Brujas y algo más/Witches and Other Things* (1984), *Women of Smoke* (1988), *Zones of Pain* (1988), *Hogueras/Bonfires* (1990), *Sargasso* (1993), *Toward the Splendid City* (1994), and *Lluvia en el desierto/Rain in the Desert* (1999). Agosín's collection of prose poems, *Circles of Madness: Mothers of the Plaza de Mayo* (1992), was illustrated with photographs of the mothers of the disappeared and other grim scenes from Argentina.

For the past decade, Agosín has concentrated on a series of critically acclaimed memoirs of her family. *La Felicidad*, first published in Santiago, was her first prose collection to be published in English. Translated as *Happiness* (1994), it could easily qualify as "magical realism," but Agosín's work goes beyond that shop-worn term. As Elena Poniatowska wrote, "Marjorie Agosín could well be the creator of a new fantastic literature in Latin America." *A Cross and a Star: Memoirs of a Jewish Girl in Chile* (1995) focused on the life of Agosín's mother in the small town of Osorno, Chile, under a generally unknown Nazi regime. This was followed by *Always from Somewhere Else: A Memoir of My Chilean Jewish Father* (1998). She has also written an autobiography, *The Alphabet in My Hands: A Writing Life* (2000).

Agosín is also the editor of *A Dream of Light & Shadow: Portraits of Latin American Women Writers* (1995), *Tapestries of Hope, Threads of Love: The Arpillera Movement in Chile, 1974-1994* (1996), *The House of Memory: Jewish Stories for Jewish Women of Latin America* (1999), and *A Map of Hope: Women Writers and Human Rights* (1999).

Agosín is the Luella Lamer Slain Professor of Latin American Studies at Wellesley College, where she is adored by her students

About the Translator

Laura Rocha Nakazawa was born and raised in Montevideo, Uruguay. Her medical studies in Montevideo were interrupted by widespread civil unrest and resistance that followed the takeover of Uruguay's government by a military junta in 1973. Nakazawa participated in the student resistance movement to the military dictatorship, and in 1974 emigrated to the United States. She subsequently pursued a career as a translator and interpreter, a craft that she learned from her father, a journalist and diplomat. Nakazawa's work spans several diverse fields and activities, encompassing both language and engagement with social and humanitarian issues. Her collaboration with Marjorie Agosín includes the translation of a significant body of Agosín's poetry into English. Nakazawa lives in Wellesley, Massachusetts, with her husband and three daughters.

About the Author of the Introduction

Robert Bonazzi has written extensively about Latin American literature, the history of American racism, and contemporary American poetry. He has written essays on Marjorie Agosín and Latin American writing for *Bloomsbury Review*, *The National Catholic Reporter*, *San Francisco Book Review*, *Southwest Review*, *Texas Observer* and *Vortex*, among other journals and magazines.

His Latitudes Press imprint (1966-2000) published work by such Latin American masters as Jorge Luis Borges, Macedonio Fernández, Octavio Paz, Juan José Arreola, Gabriel García-Márquez, Enrique Lihn, Oscar Hahn, Jaime Sabines, José Emilio Pacheco and Julio Ortega.

As Literary Executor for The Estate of John Howard Griffin, he edited six volumes of Griffin's work: *Black Like Me* and *Street of the Seven Angels* for Wings Press; *Scattered Shadows: A Memoir of Blindness and Vision* and *Follow the Ecstasy* for Orbis Books; *Encounters with the Other* and *Pilgrimage* for Latitudes. His *Man in the Mirror*, a study of *Black Like Me*, was published in 1997 by Orbis (fourth printing, 2004).

Author of four books of poetry, his work has appeared in over 200 publications in the US, UK, France, Germany, Canada, Mexico and Peru. Forthcoming titles: *The Scribbling Cure*: Texts for Three Hands and *Maestro of Solitude*: Selected Poems, 1970-2005. He writes an occasional column on poetry, *Poetic Diversity*, for the *San Antonio Express-News*.

Acknowledgments

"Passover in Chile" first appeared in *Moment Magazine* (Spring 2003). "Las cosas olvidadas," "Paz," and "El arbol de la memoria" first appeared in *Bridges* (Vol. X, no. 2, Autumn, 2005). "Sebastopol" first appeared in *Kestrell* (No. 18, Fall 2005).

Translation of *Among the Angels of Memory / Entre los ángeles de la memoria* was made possible in part by a generous grant from Wellesley College, Wellesley, Massachusetts.

Wings Press was founded in 1975 by Joanie Whitebird and Joseph F. Lomax, both deceased, as "an informal association of artists and cultural mythologists dedicated to the preservation of the literature of the nation of Texas." The publisher/editor since 1995, Bryce Milligan is honored to carry on and expand that mission to include the finest in American writing, without commercial considerations clouding the choice to publish or not to publish. Technically a "for profit" press, Wings receives only occasional underwriting from individuals and institutions who wish to support our vision. For this we are very grateful.

Wings Press attempts to produce multicultural books, chapbooks, CDs, DVDs and broadsides that, we hope, enlighten the human spirit and enliven the mind. Everyone ever associated with Wings has been or is a writer, and we know well that writing is a transformational art form capable of changing the world, primarily by allowing us to glimpse something of each other's souls. Good writing is innovative, insightful, and interesting. But most of all it is honest.

Likewise, Wings Press is committed to treating the planet itself as a partner. Thus the press uses as much recycled material as possible, from the paper on which the books are printed to the boxes in which they are shipped.

The author of the introduction to this volume, Robert Bonazzi, is also an old hand in the small press world, long the publisher / editor of Latitudes Press (1966-2000). Bonazzi and Milligan share a commitment to independent publishing and have collaborated on numerous projects over the past 25 years. As Robert Dana wrote in *Against the Grain*, "Small press publishing is personal publishing. In essence, it's a matter of personal vision, personal taste and courage, and personal friendships." Welcome to our world.

Colophon

This first edition of *Among the Angels of Memory / Entre los ángeles de la memoria*, by Marjorie Agosín, has been printed on 70 pound non-acidic paper containing fifty percent recycled fiber. Text and poem titles have been set using Adobe Caslon type; book titles in Parisian ICG type. The first 50 signature sets to be pulled from the press have been numbered and signed by the author. Wings Press books are designed by Bryce Milligan.